A DEVOTIONAL

FOOTBALL LIFE JESUS

RANDY ALLIGOOD

HIGHERLIFE
PUBLISHING & MARKETING

Published by: HigherLife Development Services, Inc.
PO Box 623307
Oviedo, FL 32762
(407) 563-4806
www.ahigherlife.com

CONTENTS

FOREWORD

I was having breakfast with Troy, a pastor at a local church who also served as a chaplain at the local high school. As a part-time football coach at a small Christian high school, as well as someone touched by the gospel, I was especially interested in his work as a chaplain. It seemed to me, maybe incorrectly so, that chaplains would be happy to have some ideas for devotions to share with the players. I decided to write down some of the things I had been saying to my football team, in an effort to connect football concepts to life and God.

I love football. More than that, I love communicating what I have learned over the years as to why the gospel is good news. Just about every day at practice I would connect a football principle with a life principle and ultimately the gospel. To help guys like Troy and any others who believe football is a great teacher of life and who want to go deeper than X's and O's, I decided to write down some of what I had been communicating.

I have also noticed over the years of coaching that there are many coaches out there who really love their players and want so much to help them succeed in life. This book is for them too.

And, of course, dads, moms, other relatives, and friends play such an important role in the life and success of an athlete. This book will help you train the heart and mind for godliness. Scripture says that "physical training is of some value, but godliness has value for all things" (1 Tim. 4:8). Frankly, I think we spend too much time thinking about ourselves, mostly about how we measure up, how good we are, how bad we are, how mad we are, and so on. But, spiritual training comes from knowing and banking on the work of Christ, from the beginning, now, and forever. Spiritual maturity means thinking more about Him in amazement than thinking about us and our plans. Therefore, I do my best to point you to Christ.

I am grateful for the opportunity to share these short devotions with you. Like the Bible says, there is nothing new under the sun (Eccl. 1:9). Nothing you are about to read is original. Most of it comes from other coaches and books I have read, as well as from my own experiences. It is likely organized a little differently than it is in other sources and includes a lot of my own stories and experiences. If you like, it should be easy for you to insert your experiences in place of mine to better illustrate the point I make. Feel free to do so.

May God bless you in your endeavor to come alongside your athlete to establish a successful heart and mind.

HOW TO USE THIS BOOK

This book is designed to help the reader teach or assist an athlete. Obviously, it can help the reader, but I have found that if I know I am going to be sharing something with someone, then my own understanding of it will need to reach a deeper level. Therefore, please enjoy this book with an eye toward helping someone else.

Each chapter starts with a principle relating to football. In a sense, I answered the question, "What is it that every coach wants from his player?" You can repeat this teaching segment with your athlete. Have fun with this part!

After the football principle, there is a life principle. The life principle connects to the football principle. There is usually a story involved. If you come up with your own story to illustrate this point, it will be much more powerful. After this point is shared, ask questions: What is the point? How does it apply in real life? Can you think of a situation going on right now in your life where this principle is applicable? Be a facilitator; let the athlete do most of the talking, but make them think.

After the life principle, there is a spiritual principle, or what I call a Jesus principle. This is where it really became fun for me. Here is where I try to communicate the good news—that God in His amazing grace has done something for us that we can't do for ourselves. This is the part where by faith we add to our life. In this part, I am aiming at faith modification, not necessarily behavior modification. I would be so thankful if the athlete says, "Wow, I didn't know God did that for me. I can quit trying to do that for myself and simply trust in Him. I love God more because of what He has done for me!"

From time to time, I will be adding devotions and, if you like, you will be notified when I do so. Just sign up at FootballLifeandJesus.com. I won't sell any of your info or contact you because of anything.

Enjoy the good news!!!

NOTE FROM THE AUTHOR

A while back, my daughter told me that the more broken we are, the more Jesus' light shines through the cracks. Maybe that is her paraphrase of 2 Corinthians 12:9-10 where Paul is delighting in his weaknesses so that Christ's power can rest on him. Paul concludes that when he is weak, then he is strong as a result of Christ's power.

When someone writes a book, the impression might be that the author has it all together. I know I have felt that way before. I hope you don't get that impression here. As a matter of fact, I hope you get the opposite impression. I hope you get the impression that this author has so many weaknesses and questions that he needs to find strength and answers in Christ.

This book is a product of my weakness, God's spirit within me guiding me into truth, and others pouring into me. Without the weakness of my humanity, a personal guide within me and others, I would have no need or desire to share the good news on the following pages.

ONE

LISTEN UP!

Football Principle—Listen to the Coach

When I started coaching high school football, I asked the guys to listen to me. Ask too much and your players get discouraged. Ask too little and they get discouraged. Because listening is a huge challenge, I knew asking them to listen was not too little of an ask and I hoped not too much. I felt that I had a lot to say and if they just listened, then things would fall in place. By "listen," I of course meant, "listen to learn."

Prior to coaching high school football, I coached Pop Warner. So, there I was in my last year of Pop Warner as an assistant coach for Rob. I admired Rob a lot. I was listening to learn most of the time with him. He had it all—an imposing presence; eloquent and humorous speech; comebacks that made you shake your head and smile; extreme athleticism; the gift of years; football credentials from high school, Division I college, and the NFL; and even a Super Bowl ring. One day he was explaining role assignments for our 5-3 defense. Were the kids listening? Yes and no. They heard him, but most of them weren't into it. But he had a great deal to say and he said it so well. Rob was trying to impart an understanding of the game. There were a few kids who wanted to understand, but most just wanted to get to the fun stuff.

If they were ever going to listen to anyone, it should be Rob. So why didn't they? Could it be there were too many voices in their heads? Could it be they tried to listen at different levels but heard too many voices and couldn't distinguish which ones were important? Could it be they didn't trust what was being said? Perhaps an internal war of voices was drowning out the voice that most needed to be heard.

In football, the voices of apathy, laziness, and hardship war against the voices of endurance, might, and power. The voice of "I can't" wars against the voice of effort. The voices of selfishness and doubt war against the voice of commitment to playing our role and doing our job. The voice of whether we think the coach likes us wars against the voices of encouragement and acceptance. The voice of fear wars against the voice of belief. Too many voices in the huddle war against a clear play call. The voice of distracting signals from the defense wars against clear thinking for the offense. The voices of "parent agents" sometimes war against the voice that is best for the team.

When I started coaching Pop Warner, I quickly learned the "no play." The quarterback (QB) calls the play count, but the center never snaps the ball. The play is designed to make the defense jump offside resulting in a 5-yard penalty against the defense. It happens when the defense is listening to the wrong voice. They shouldn't be listening to the voice of the QB but should instead be watching the ball.

Most coaching is simply weeding out the bad voices in the players' heads and directing their attention and loyalty to the correct voice. Our job as a coach is to have a voice that is clear, consistent, and simple. A voice that is easy to listen to. A voice that is easy to follow if the player so chooses. A voice they can trust.

I like to coach the heart. When a player isn't listening or doesn't follow my instructions, I will stop everything and ask, "Do you trust me?" They have the freedom to say no. And then I can ask further, "Why don't you trust me?" And then the real learning begins.

Life Principle—Distinguish the Voices and Pick the Trustworthy One

These days it seems there are millions of voices whispering and yelling at us all at the same time (peer approval, sports figures, notoriety, girls, unrest at home, video games, TV, to name just a few). There are so many voices. They create so much confusion. When we are confused, we lack confidence and are burdened. When we are confused and burdened, we are not decisive and can't move with speed. We are robbed of our goals, inspiration, and dreams.

It is important to know what voice to trust. It is important to resist the voices that compete with the trustworthy voice.

When I was a kid, just about every afternoon we played pickup tackle football in a lot by a church down the road. When it was time for dinner, my mother would whistle, loudly. That was the voice that said, "Come home and eat." There were many times another voice would pop in my head saying, "Just keep playing; you can say you didn't hear her." There were other distractions and voices along the way home, too. But I knew my mother's voice—the whistle.

When I started dating, I somehow expected all my relationships to be like the romantic songs of the '70s. "Then Came You." "Brown-Eyed Girl." "Pretty Woman." You get the point. Those voices were powerful in my heart and head. Each relationship seemed to start fine but eventually the romance and excitement fizzled. It turns out I was listening to the wrong voice about relationships. Consequently, my relationships had no chance.

Many of us suffer from the voice of the shiny object. That's the voice that says, "Hey, check out this opportunity!" As soon as we think we want to commit to one opportunity, another comes along—another shiny object. Then we are distracted with too many opportunities, and consequently, nothing gets accomplished. Each of the opportunities is great in and of itself, but we must choose to listen to each one instead of picking one to commit to and finish.

We have to know how to recognize the right voice. We have to pick a voice to listen to and trust. There are some voices who care about us. Most voices only care about themselves.

Have you chosen the voice you will listen to? Do you like the voices in your head? Do they have your best interests at heart? Would it be worth it to find the right voices and be able to tell the wrong voices to jump in the river?

For me, I listen to the voices of the ones who give without seeking anything in return, who give sacrificially and freely, and who care about me. The voice of fear is the worst for me. The voices of defeat, discouragement, shame, guilt, discontentment, fame, and fortune are next in line. And then there are the voices that try to haunt me and my players before, during, and after the game—*you are tired, you haven't had enough time to prepare, some of your key players are hurt*—excuse after excuse, all based on fear of losing versus the joy of competing and getting better because of it. As a coach, one of my jobs is to determine what voices my players are listening to and steer them to the right one —the voice that makes them light and fun and sets them free.

Jesus Principle—The Voice of Christ Is the Most Trustworthy Voice, Worthy of Our Full Attention

Ultimately, the voice I have found to be most freeing, restful, adventurous, fulfilling, and trustworthy is the voice of the one the Bible calls Jesus. I want my players to listen to His voice. He is truth. Truth results in freedom. I want them to play free of all the other voices. His voice tells me that I have worth, that my sins have been forgiven and forgotten, that I have peace with God, and that I am loved regardless of how well I perform. His voice gives me peace in the storm. His voice gives me a reason to perform at my highest ability even though I may not like what I am hearing from my coach, other players, teachers, friends, and even parents or other circumstances that may be weighing me down. He provides an alternative to the voices that haven't gotten me very far. He lightens my load and eases my burdens and therefore allows me to think and act more decisively and quickly. I have a better chance of coaching and playing well when I listen to His voice. He makes the untrustworthy voices much less important to me.

In John 12:49, Jesus said that He spoke only what the Father told Him to speak. To do so, He had to be the perfect listener. He understood the "Spirit" of all things. Jesus willingly sacrificed His life for each of us. He deserves a shot at being the voice we listen to. In my experience, His voice is so trustworthy that I can ignore all other competing voices. I pray that you will give the ears of your heart and mind to Jesus so that He can whisper truth that will save you and set you free to be the best you can be. Scripture says that those who believe have been given the mind of Christ. That mind is certainly a terrible thing to waste. May we all listen to His voice.

TWO
LITTLE THINGS AND MIRACLES

Football Principle—Football Is a Big Game, but Success Comes from the Little Things

You don't have to be around football very long to hear phrases like, "It's a game of inches," or "It's always the little things that trip us up." A player lining up too far inside, missing a snap count, taking his eye off the ball, holding the ball too loosely, not hustling down the field, or running into the huddle too late are all little, seemingly mundane, things. When a coach continuously reminds his players about these things, the usual response is groaning or sighing or "I got it, I got it." It is boring and no one likes to practice against them, but every game is full of these "little" mistakes. In a close game, more often than not these little mistakes cost the game. In fact, every undesired result (i.e., a lost fumble) can be boiled down to some "little" mistake (i.e., the ball carrier didn't squeeze the ball properly).

In a spring game of ours one year, I noticed that in some of our plays, we were literally one step of extra speed from breaking off long runs for touchdowns. One little step.

When we line up it has meaning. When we huddle up it has meaning. When we have too much weight on our heels in our stance it has meaning. When a blocker steps toward the defender it has meaning. Each of these little things means something to you and to your team. One can only imagine the power of all these little things done right.

What is the root of the problem when a player or coach doesn't want to practice the little things? Could it be we don't realize how much they really mean to the outcome of the game? When we become great at the little things, the big plays come.

Life Principle—Plant Little Seeds to Grow Big Trees

At a meeting in Orlando, Florida, I heard former US Attorney General John Ashcroft say that one of the greatest gifts God has given us is the gift of consequences. Everything we do or don't do has a consequence and we have no idea the size of the consequence. Nor do we have any control over all the results. If you have ever studied game or practice film, then you know that the little things have big consequences.

Every life has meaning. Recently I heard about the "butterfly effect," which is the scientifically-proven phenomenon that the single flap of a butterfly's wing in North America could actually contribute toward a tsunami in Japan. When we do something, whether big or small, there are consequences set in motion. Whether in sports or in life, many of us don't think we matter because we haven't seen anything we have done that may qualify for greatness. We don't really know or see all the consequences of our actions, either immediate or long-range. Our life and everything we do and how we do it has meaning. Could a simple smile or maybe one act of kindness really mean the difference between life or death for millions of people?

The truth is that most of us have dreamed of doing something great and being recognized for it, of being famous for what we have done. We want to be the MVP of the Super Bowl or win the Nobel Peace Prize or go to the Olympics. Pursuing a dream is awesome, but we have to be careful not to push aside or diminish the daily "little" things that are good in and of themselves and that may result in a much greater good. There is no promise that any of us will be famous.

I bet every Super Bowl MVP, Nobel Peace Prize winner, or Olympic athlete had a mom, dad, brother, sister, or some other person who had a huge hand in making them successful, but no one knows their name. As humans, we tend to glorify the winner, but the truth is that no person has ever done anything on his own. Rather, the accomplishment is the result of the sum of many "little" contributions to that person's life orchestrated by God. One day, we will know the fruit of our "little" contributions to those around us, but until then, we can have faith that they will have meaning. Learn to support others with little things and see what big adventures unfold.

Jesus Principle—God Can Turn the Smallest Things into Mighty Miracles

The Bible says that "whoever can be trusted with very little can also be trusted with much" (Luke 16:10). When I see a player who gives his all doing footwork or intentionally focuses on lining up correctly and does the other little things right, I know I can trust that player in the big things. I know that he is a player who understands that the little things can have big meanings.

I am reminded of the biblical story of the fishes and the loaves where a little boy gave his lunch and Jesus multiplied it and fed five thousand people. Whoever made lunch for that boy that morning had no idea the few fishes and loaves would feed thousands. What a thrill it must have been for that boy to see Jesus miraculously turn a small gesture into something great.

Similarly, even if you can only give what appears to be a little, then give it.

Do not be embarrassed. Be disciplined to give regardless of how you feel. In God's economy, those who give with great effort and fullness of heart give more than those who are rich and give much more in dollars and cents but less in heart. The same is true on the field, at practice and game time. One day at practice, some of the less-gifted athletes weren't trying very hard on a particular drill because they couldn't keep up with the more athletically gifted athletes (who weren't trying that hard either). I reminded them of the story in the Bible of the poor widow who gave a mite (less than a penny) and was recognized by Jesus as giving more than the rich man, because the widow gave more based on what she had. The same is true for players. A player who has less talent but gives it all gives more than the great athlete who doesn't give his all.

The voice of the antagonist will always say, "Don't worry about the little things; focus on the big stuff; be a star; don't waste your time on the little junk; why do we keep doing the same little stuff over and over? No one will ever know if we skip this." There are many antagonists out there, including our own mind.

Instead of going with the flow and listening to the antagonist, may we be found to have been faithful in the little things and to have given much even when it is just a little. Integrity in the little things breeds trust for the big stuff and confidence that big things will happen. There is no better path to the big stuff than making sure the little stuff is done well. What if the little boy with his few fishes and loaves would have shied away from the opportunity to give what little he had to Jesus? He would not have felt the joy of watching his little offering miraculously turn into more than enough to feed five thousand people. Is it possible that giving that little extra could result in a miracle? I think so. I know so.

So, remain faithful in the little things, and continue to plant the seeds and flap your wings and give what you have to give even if you think it won't matter, and then one day you will look back on a mighty forest and great tsunami. God is the multiplier.

In fact, knowing who God is, and how few resources and little time we have to prepare and practice the little things, I have made it a habit to pray out loud in front of the players for God to triple our efforts. I love the thought that God will multiply our effort. Sometimes, it is my only hope that we will be able to perform well. God is able to do far more than we can ever imagine with whatever we offer, no matter how little.

THREE
NEVER GIVE UP

Football Principle—Be Selfish, Don't Give Up, Regardless of the Scoreboard

I was so impressed with our basketball team as I stood there and watched our players dive for balls and risk injury with a high-energy offense and a gritty defense until the last second of the game. We lost by sixty. Those kids inspired me to start the football program at the International Community School. Most of the basketball players would also play football and they had no "quit" in them. I felt like we could easily lose all of our football games our first year. Honestly, I was thinking all I could ask for was a few first downs and maybe a score or two. But these kids were playing for more than the scoreboard. Continuous, competitive effort was important to them.

I have to say that one of the saddest things I have seen is when a player gives up—discouraged, beaten, and totally yielded, without spirit. It has happened to me in the past. I regret those times.

Have you ever seen a team practically fold after an easy start, or when they are so far ahead, but the other team either wins or comes close to winning? I have some bad memories of those games as a fan, coach, and player. I am not talking about the times at the end of the game when we put in the second string and watched our big lead get a little smaller. Rather, I am talking about when the team had a presumption that "we are going to win" because winning is in our control; or when a premature celebration causes us to lose the sharpness of our edge; or when a reduced intensity eventually leads to a loss on the scoreboard or at least a close call. That overconfidence and reduced intensity is a different kind of giving up than the giving up that just walks away discouraged. But I believe both kinds of giving up have the same underlying causes.

There are several reasons why we give up:

1. **We don't understand the meaning or purpose of competition.** As I understand it, competition began for the sole purpose of honing skills and getting better. The whole purpose was to be better when you were finished competing than when you started. Although the competitors competed to win, they did so in order to master their skills, not for bragging rights. In fact, "com-," the prefix of "compete" means "with." Competitors competed "with" one another, not "against" one another. If one competes to get better, then they try hard regardless of the circumstances. If they are better at the end of the competition, then they are successful, regardless of the scoreboard. And, on top of all that, they have the satisfaction of helping someone else get better.

2. **We play more for the outcome than anything else.** A logical extension of competing "with" rather than "against" one another is that we shouldn't play too much for the outcome. I cringe when I hear a coach say that a win is a win regardless of how they played. That view is short-term and shallow, in my opinion. I love it when I hear, "I want us to play well, and the scoreboard will take care of itself." The fact is there are so many things that determine the outcome that we don't control. Let's play to win because we know that in order to win, we have to play well. But we shouldn't play just to win as if winning is the end of it. If outcomes control us, then our life is a rollercoaster. It is hard to coach or play under either extreme. Think about it.

If we are focused on the outcome, we are not focused on execution or the job at hand. Don't rely on the scoreboard for comfort. Take comfort in intense preparation, effort, and execution down to the last play of the game.

3. **We think winning is everything.** There are few folks who remember who won which games last year and even fewer who will remember the scores. And at some point, no one will remember. Records of wins and losses are forgotten as generations come and go. Usually, even the person or team who holds the record understands over time that the record has added little to their true self-worth. Each new generation has their own heroes and the previous generation's heroes are remembered but not revered. The glory of winning fades. It is not enough to satisfy our souls in the long run.

4. **We have not absorbed the greatest motivation of all.** More on that later.

Life Principle—Overcome the Temptation to Give Up. It's about the Journey

I remember vividly walking down the hallway of our home in Orlando holding my baby son. He was crying his eyes out and there was nothing I could do about it. It was me or him. Who was going to give in first? Two hours later he fell asleep. I gently laid him in his crib. I remember that night because it was hard, very hard, but I didn't give up and get angry or frustrated. I stayed in the game and cared the whole way through. I loved him. I did not want to give up on him, no matter the circumstances.

Giving up on my son that night and letting him cry it out on his own at the other end of the house would have been much easier, but I knew that hard times would come with him and the other kids and that I had to learn not to give up.

All relationships are difficult at times, whether they are with spouses, kids, extended family, bosses, employees, friends, teachers, or anyone else. Relationships require work. It goes against my goals in life just to write people off. My overall goal in life is to see to it that no one misses the grace of God. I want people to have the advantage of knowing Christ and experiencing the richness that comes with Him.

While people and relationships can be the most tempting to give up on, our dreams, passions, and endeavors are a close second.

Law school exams were four hours long. The difference between an A and B was the ability to stay in the game the last hour. To care, to keep striving. To not give in to the negative voices. To try hard until the bell. Not giving up paid off and the good grades helped me land a good job in Atlanta.

But the good job was yet another challenge. There were so many reasons to quit my first law job, but I am glad I didn't give up. While it was an unpleasant place to be, I learned many valuable lessons that help me to this day.

In the life cycle of our dreams, I believe many of us give up too soon. The vision we have remains just an idea. We give up before giving all we have to give and before we learn the lessons that make us more prepared for our future. If we learn something valuable, then we win, regardless of whether the original dream comes true.

In one of the most famous speeches ever, Winston Churchill, the prime minister of England at the time England was struggling at war with Nazi Germany, emphasized over and over again the importance of never giving in.

Don't get me wrong. There is a time to roll on in life, even in relationships and dreams. But most of us don't explore all the options of staying in the game. Most of us don't give all that we have to give, most of us don't seek wise counsel, and most of us fear giving and then failing.

If it is about the journey and not only about the outcome, then we can experience many victories along the way. If nothing else, learning to persevere is a major victory.

Jesus Principle—

A. God Never Gives Up on Me

Scripture says that while we were God's enemies, He demonstrated His love for us and sent His Son to die for us (Rom. 5:8). Scripture is clear that His grace overcomes all of our faults and shortcomings. It doesn't matter the quantity or the magnitude of our wrongdoing. Jesus paid it all and finished the sin issue. Remember the prodigal son and his father? What a beautiful picture of mistake after mistake, but the father never gave up on the wayward son. The father never said, "You are no longer my son." In fact, when the father saw the wayward son approaching, the father ran to him. The act of the father running was highly dishonoring in that culture, but the father cared more about his son than what others thought. What a beautiful demonstration of God pursuing us.

Colossians 3:23 says to employees and anyone else working under the authority of another to work heartily as if unto the Lord, not unto men. I used that verse in football to communicate the message to never give up. If we work unto men (or women), then they will eventually fail us or do us wrong. The same is true if we work unto ourselves. But God has never disappointed us and never will. God loves us perfectly. When we attach ourselves to His love, even fear is cast out.

The Bible says love never ends. That means it never gives in or gives up. Since God never gives up on us, then is there any reason we should give up on what He has called us to do? When all is failing and I am tempted to give up, I have to remind myself that God will never give up on me. That type of love deserves my best all the time regardless of the scoreboard or any other circumstances. When we play as if unto Him, we have no reason to give up! His love and what He has done for us is the greatest motivator of all. In His presence, we are completely free and loved regardless of our failures, mistakes, and losses. That is a perfect recipe for playing our best with all of our heart regardless of the score—a perfect recipe for persevering, for never giving up.

B. It Is Okay to Give Up Certain Things

It is true that God will never give up on us. However, it is also true that God will give us over to our sinful desires. Just as the prodigal son was allowed to move on and choose his own way, regardless of how destructive it was, we are allowed to choose our own way. Too bad. I would much rather be able to turn on a switch that would prevent me from choosing the wrong way. The only switch we have is to yield to the Spirit. Even if we choose incorrectly, God welcomes us with open arms. The prodigal son finally humbled himself and came home to his father's love.

Similarly, there are certain things we should give up on, from a spiritual perspective, like trying to be a better Christian. Let me explain. From my perspective, for such a long time I thought the Christian life was much like playing football—working hard to get better. Add to that, stay right with God; please God; keep short accounts with God; confess, confess, *confess*; you aren't living good enough to be blessed; God will get you for that; if I do this or that, then God will bless me. Well, the good news of the gospel is: *Give up on all that!!!*

It is so easy to be deceived into thinking and believing those lies. In fact, in many ways, the world works this way. But God does not. The fact is when we receive His Son, He (not us) is the one who works in us, He gives us righteousness as a gift, and makes us right with Him, simply as a result of the work of His amazing Son. He also gave us the gift of forgiveness. We are forgiven by faith in the work of His Son. Yet another gift is that God isn't angry with us and He is not looking to "get even" with us. Simply as a result of the work of Christ, we are not condemned and the wrath of God has no place in our lives (Rom. 8:1–2).

Life is hard enough. Why add God to your list of burdens? Give up on believing the way the world says your relationship with God should be and believe the way God says it should be. Give up and let God be the giver. He is the giver and we are the receiver. He simply wants us to take by faith all that He has to give, and then give it away.

FOUR
NO REGRETS

Football Principle—Chest Out, Chin Up, No Regrets

More times than not, the kids who cry after a loss are the ones who didn't give it their all, for whatever reason. My regrets in life have usually been because I didn't really commit my all to what I was doing. My lack of commitment was the result of fear, laziness, hoping in hope without reason, making emotional decisions, impatience or arrogance, and the list goes on ... all character flaws.

Ben cried after the only win his team had last season. In this case, he cried because he had worked so hard and spent so much energy and never gave up or stopped believing. He cried because he had given it his all. So, the opposite is true as well. No regrets, just joy, when we give it our all.

The hardest kids to coach are the ones who pretend to give it their all—the players who are clearly holding themselves back, the ones who aren't willing to rebel against fear and take a risk. Is it because when we give everything we have we are afraid it won't be good enough? So, we hold some back, just to have an excuse? I am sure there are many reasons.

Before the game begins, picture yourself after the game drenched in sweat, worn out and dirty, but with your chest out and chin up as you walk across the field to shake hands with the other team. Imagine yourself being completely satisfied with your effort and having no regret.

The bottom line is that at the end of every play, every game, every practice, every drill, every chalk talk, and every season, we want to look back and say with pride, "I have no regrets." It will take a lot of effort throughout the season. It is a challenge to push ourselves each moment to give all we can, to unleash all that we have to offer. But the reward is restful, including no regret. The opposite of regret is satisfaction and joy. Satisfaction and joy are worth fighting for.

Life Principle—Failure Is Only Regretful If We Don't Give One Hundred Percent

There is something truly freeing about giving more than we are comfortable giving—emotionally, physically, and mentally. When we give all we have, what else is there that can be done? What is left to regret? It doesn't mean we can't do better the next time. Our best can certainly get better, with hard work, rethinking, and practice. Giving our best at any given moment produces a rest and a hilarity in our soul. When we give it our all, whatever the outcome, we can smile and say in our heart, "Okay," and stand proud regardless of the outcome.

When we hide behind excuses and explanations for not giving our all, at least part of the regret comes from never knowing how good we can be. When we strive for maximum effort, there is something that rises within us to be better next time, and we usually are better next time. When we don't give everything, we are only left with the hollow illusion that we could have done it.

A willingness to fail is freeing. It can even be fun. When Edison invented the light bulb, he failed hundreds of times. His view, however, was that he had learned hundreds of ways how not to make a light bulb. If we can view failure as a learning experience, then we win even when we fail.

Maximum effort is at least in part an adventure, and the end of that adventure is rarely regret.

Jesus Principle—Pursuing Christ Is a Guarantee Against Regret

A man named Paul had an encounter with Christ and his life turned around 180 degrees. Through him, God did many great things including starting the early churches and writing most of the New Testament. Paul lost everything to gain Christ because he considered the cause of Christ to be greater than any earthly treasures. He no doubt lived a full life. At the end of his life, he remarked, "I have fought the good fight, I have finished the race, I have kept the faith" (2 Tim. 4:7). He was a man without regrets even though he eventually gave his life for his beliefs. He lost his life to gain life. In each of our endeavors can we say, "I have fought the good fight"?

The truth is we will have days where we don't give it our all. There is only one person who always gave it His all—Jesus. For a sinless being to voluntarily and lovingly die for the sinful is the ultimate example of giving everything. Fortunately, for those of us who believe in Him, He resides in us and continues to give us His all. We must receive it by faith.

Focus on the one who gave His all, the one Paul said lives in and through those who believe, and see what happens. I have never regretted the times that I know I had nothing left to offer and allowed Christ to simply live through me. For me to give all that I have, because I have Christ in me, I must give Him to others.

Because Christ gave it all, why can't we give our all by continuously opening our hearts and receiving from Him? There will be no regrets when we keep our eyes fixed on Him and keep the faith.

FIVE

SEEK UNDERSTANDING

Football Principle—Understanding Plus Effort Is Greater than Effort Alone

If you have two teams of equal talent and skill, but one has a deeper understanding of the game, who will come out on top?

I love it when a player stops me in the middle of teaching time and asks, "What about this or that?" It tells me they are trying to understand what is going on. They are interested in the concepts, the meaning, the why, the reason we are doing what we are doing. They want to know more than "this is where I line up when you call this play." They want to know why lining up in that certain place gives us a better chance of success.

Our first offense was designed for quick-hitting runs. My tailback had previously played in an offense designed for him to look for the hole after the handoff. He was used to lining up about eight yards back, starting off slow, and then bursting to the hole. I wanted him only five yards behind the QB. I wanted him to hit the assigned hole quickly and at maximum speed because our blocking scheme was designed to give him a quick opening that typically would not stay open long. When he finally understood the timing and the design, he was successful. He ran for a lot of yards after he developed a deeper understanding of our scheme.

A deep understanding often requires some struggle and extra work. If a player goes the extra mile and puts in the time to understand not just his role but the roles of those around him in every play, then he becomes more valuable to the team and to the coach. Understanding the big picture and all the details within it are critical to success.

I believe a deep understanding of the game is one of the primary qualities that separates the great from the good. Earnestly seek to understand everything you can about your coach, your teammates, and your scheme. Ask a zillion questions. Study game film. Learn. You will be better and everyone around you will be better because of you. And who knows what doors will open for you?

Life Principle—It Doesn't Hurt to Ask Why; In Fact, It Helps

I make my living by practicing law. I have made it a point to understand my client's business better than they do. Not just the law applicable to their business but the business side as well. I will ask myself, for example, what influences their bottom line the most? In some cases, I have been able to save and/or add to the bottom-line millions of dollars. These clients generally don't mind paying their bill. This wasn't always the case, though. Early in my career, I worked hard for long hours, but I only did what I was told, not much more. I was more or less an order-taker. After I was fired, I woke up and decided to take ownership of what I was doing and understand the "why." Everything turned around.

I have had "order-takers" work for me. In most cases, they really wanted to please me and our clients, which is good, but only taking orders doesn't help me beyond a superficial level. An "order-taker" generally thinks the creative thought process is over and they just do what they're told. They don't bring much extra value to the issue at hand. They don't seek to understand the "why."

I recently gave some edits on a contract that I discovered later were incorrect. Without asking why I made those edits or checking behind me, he just gave them to the assistant to type in. I then gave him my "why" speech and now he is going deeper. He was pleased to learn I wanted to know what he thinks about things.

About ten years ago, we took our family to Branson, Missouri, for a family camp. In the morning, my wife, Jennifer, and I would go to mini-conferences while the kids were zip-lining, rock climbing, and shooting arrows. The topic that week for the married adults was dispute resolution. My one takeaway from the entire week was to seek understanding. I may not agree with Jennifer on every point, but I need to seek to understand her point of view. Seeking understanding requires asking questions and then listening. The times when I have sidelined my point of view and sought to understand hers has made me smarter and easier to get along with, and it has often revealed some deeper issue that we both wanted to fix.

In the Book of Proverbs, we hear over and over again the admonition to "seek understanding." We are to seek it like we would seek gold. We are told it is more valuable than rubies. That means we are to seek it tenaciously and with perseverance and determination.

My advice—wrestle and fight to understand, until whatever you are after has been simplified in your mind, until you can teach it to a fifth grader. Only then do you have understanding, one that will benefit you and those around you and last a lifetime.

Jesus Principle—The "Why" of Jesus Is Love

Is the same not true for our spiritual life? Why does God say what He says in the Bible? When we understand that, then the whole world opens up to us. Why did God do what He did? Why did He send Jesus? Why is grace necessary? What is the meaning of "the last will be first and the first will be last" or "we must lose our life to find it"? (Matt. 20:16; Matt. 10:39).

As I have walked the Christian journey, it has become more and more clear to me that all things were created by, for, and through Christ, and God's motivation for all things has been and continues to be His immeasurable love for us. The big picture is Christ Himself and all the details flow for His glory.

We certainly have a distinct advantage, as believers, to understand the things of God. The Bible says that when we put our faith in Christ and believe in Him for salvation, God puts His Spirit within us as a permanent seal of salvation. The Spirit gives us the mind of Christ to understand spiritual things that cannot be understood by the natural mind. For example, in Ephesians 3:14–21, Paul prayed that the power of the Spirit will help us understand how wide and high and deep is the love of God for us. We also learn that living in the power of the Spirit means that we actually do understand the magnitude of that love. I had always thought that walking in the Spirit or being filled with the Spirit meant that I had extra Superman powers to do things; and frankly, because of that erroneous belief, I felt somewhat inadequate. I had never realized that walking in the Spirit meant to be so filled up with love that my cup runs over to all those around me; it's a love that only God can give. How freeing.

SIX
PASSION

Football Principle—Suffer for Success

A coach wants a player who is willing to give up some things in their life in pursuit of playing better. It certainly helps if the coach is not the only one making sacrifices. Examples of sacrifices that might result in better play include extra practice time instead of TV time; going to bed at a reasonable hour rather than staying up so late; hanging out with folks who are like-minded rather than folks who might be entertaining but who are always in trouble; watching film of next week's opponent rather than playing video games; turning work in on time rather than texting or Snapchatting so much; eating vegetables and good proteins rather than too much candy; drinking water and juices rather than sodas … and the list goes on. These sacrifices bring value to any athlete. Do we want to be the best we can be?

In my first year of coaching (also the first year of our team's football program), we desperately needed a tailback and a middle linebacker. I prayed to the Lord to give us a couple of kids who could meet those needs. The Lord answered that prayer when two kids from a local public school decided to come to our little private school. The tailback made a significant contribution the first year (as did the linebacker), but I knew he had more to give. The second season he got better and better as the year went along. At the end of the season, he was one of the best running backs in the conference. At some point late in the season, he told me that he was waking up every morning and doing pushups and footwork ladder drills. He sacrificed a little sleep time in the morning to become a better player. This was his passion, his sacrifice. I loved it and was inspired by it. He realized his potential and received a college scholarship. It was worth the sacrifice.

A couple years ago in a postgame huddle, the coach of an opposing team pleaded with his players to start working out with weights and to spend more time becoming stronger and faster. He was really asking for passion— for their sacrifice to become better players. He knew it would make them better players and better persons. But without their passion, their willingness to give up something else, it would mean very little.

How is passion developed? Is passion something that just happens? Where would you like your passions to land? Do you like where you are in your heart? Would you like to be better? Are you tired of knowing in your heart you can do better but not doing it? Are you on one of those teams that loses games you probably could win if there had been a little more sacrifice early on? Are you tired of saying, "I could do that if I wanted to"? Are you satisfied with just having "potential" without results? Are you simply sitting comfortably based on your past accomplishments, or are you measuring your actions based on your potential? These are all good questions for our souls and may lead us to find value in the suffering part of passion.

Life Principle—Got Passion?

We don't have to think too long to identify our passions. Just ask, what am I willing to sacrifice my time and/or money or other opportunities for? We all have passions. Even someone who sleeps and watches TV all day has a passion for those things, because he is willing to give up other opportunities for them. Taking a little time to identify our passions and what we are sacrificing to follow those passions is a good exercise.

When I was a kid, one of my passions was eating cheese sandwiches and watching TV. No kidding. Sounds cheesy, I know. I spent a lot of time sitting on the couch by myself eating cheese sandwiches and watching TV. If only I had thought about the things I was giving up— the possibility of making new friends, of participating in a sport, of learning something new, of being part of a cause bigger than me (whatever that might be), then maybe I would have made some different choices.

Those choices perhaps would have changed the object of my passion to something less comfortable, but more exciting and perhaps of more benefit to me and others, and for sure more memorable. I remember having compassion for an old man the local newspaper had identified as blind and poor. That compassion gave me a passion to help him. I remember going around my neighborhood with a cigar box to collect money for him. That passion was really my willingness to give up other things like watching TV to help someone. Today, I am glad I did that. He felt special and blessed and so did I.

For years I watched my daughter play volleyball. Year after year I struggled with the fact that I knew she could be better and that she would enjoy it more if she played to her potential. I knew she had to get stronger and quicker. She lacked core strength. She could barely do a push-up. I tried to encourage her to go with her mother to work out in the weight room at the local volleyball club where she played. For years she wasn't willing to make the sacrifice. Finally, I got tired of the fact that she wasn't enjoying volleyball as much as she could. I got tired of her complaining about falling short. I made her work out. I told her that if after three weeks she couldn't feel a positive difference in her life, then she didn't have to go anymore. A year later she was still working out and she even woke up early on Saturday morning. Working out became her passion. Her high school coaches said she improved so much. For the first time, she was one of the "go-to" girls. She enjoyed that season a great deal.

Jesus Principle—Jesus Has Passion for Us

When the movie *The Passion of the Christ* came out, it was the first time I had truly grabbed the underlying meaning of the term "passion." It was so real and so graphic. Prior to that movie, I had equated passion with some sort of focused, sometimes fierce pursuit of something or someone. Some of the greatest movies and books illustrate such a pursuit. What I learned from *The Passion of the Christ* was that the root of passion is suffering. Suffering in this context is not the suffering that occurs when we have the flu or when our house has burned down. Suffering in this context is the suffering that occurs when we are willing to give up something to get something else, a willingness to sacrifice.

I am a member of a Christian men's group called DreamBuilders. Our vision is to unleash God's dreams from the hearts of men. We define a dream as the answer to the following two questions:

1. Who do I want to help?
2. How do I want to help them?

One of our leader's dreams is to help everyone understand how big and powerful and passionate God really is. One way he set out to do this was by creating an annual event on the last Saturday in June called Join the Applause, where everyone around the world is invited to go outside and ponder God's creation, to view it as a gift from God, as a concert orchestrated by God as the artist and us as the audience member. And to understand that the Creator is bigger than the creation.

Join the Applause is a twenty-four-hour event starting in the first time zone in New Zealand. As the sun sets around the world people applaud an awesome God for His wondrous works, for His passion for His Son (for whom all things were created), and ultimately for us. The event has been going on for a few years, and each year I regret not inviting more people to participate in this worldwide celebration. In some years I am more passionate about this event than in other years. I always know how passionate I am by the amount of money and time I am willing to spend on inviting folks to join the celebration. Thanking God is a passion that I want to grow in my heart. I am confident it will grow as God continues to remind me that He is passionate for me.

I have wondered what it means in Scripture when Peter says he was overjoyed to participate in the sufferings of Christ (1 Pet. 4:13). Christ was misunderstood. Those in authority and those who followed Him were thinking He had come for a power play—to overthrow the government and rescue the Jews. He suffered because He was misunderstood. So then, when we are misunderstood in our good deeds and sharing of the gospel, are we not participating in the sufferings of Christ? Also, Christ loved the unlovely. Loving the unlovely and those who fight against our love is difficult. Are we not participating in the sufferings of Christ when we love the unlovely? We should all pray that God would give us a passion for the unlovely so that we would be willing to sacrifice and suffer for them.

Scripture says that when we delight in God, He gives us the desires of our heart (Ps. 37:4). Based on this promise, I try to delight in God when faced with a decision, and then I listen to my heart's desire. Many times, that desire is the seed of a new passion and almost always involves helping someone.

I pray that we will view God as passionate toward us and that God will help us identify our passions and give us new passions through which He can bless us and others through us beyond our wildest imagination. Passion makes sacrifice taste better.

SEVEN

DISCIPLINE—FAITHFUL IN THE LITTLE THINGS

Football Principle—Discipline Means Faithful in the Little Things

Spring of 2012 was our high school football team's first game ever. Practicing the fundamentals had gone pretty well, but now we were up against resistance. We were up against an extremely physical and well-established football team. Yes, we got trounced and no, we didn't get a first down or any points, but we were not humiliated or discouraged. In fact, it was a building point for our program. Why? Because we proved we could do the little things well and I knew that those little things would lead to big things. Everyone lined up perfectly each time, our stances were good, we didn't jump offsides, we had no confusion on play calls, we knew our assignments, and aside from simply being outmatched, we executed well. Generally, the things we could control went well. We showed that we were capable of being disciplined. At the end of the game, a boy from another school who came to watch the game decided to come to our school and play. What a compliment to our team. Frankly, I couldn't believe he wanted to play for us. It was a miracle and I was very thankful.

I pick up pennies. Do I need to do so to feed my family? Maybe one day, but it does not appear that way now. The reason I pick up pennies is because it is a great reminder that little things add up, and I am never above stooping low to pick up something even only slightly meaningful. There is a verse in the Bible that says, "Whoever can be trusted with very little can also be trusted with much" (Luke 16:10). I have always wanted to be faithful in the big things, and I want to constantly demonstrate that I am faithful in the little things. As a coach, I look for the players who pay attention to the little things—the ones who don't skip corners when they run laps, the ones who go all the way down and up on their push-ups, the ones who run all the way to the end of the drill rather than slowing down, the ones who start over when they get it wrong. I know I can trust those players with bigger roles and when the game is on the line.

Sometimes it is helpful simply to define something. Discipline has many meanings and connotations. Let's define discipline as an attitude to make sure we do the little things well.

Life Principle—Discipline Is a Springboard for Beauty and Adventure

It takes discipline and integrity to pay attention to the little things, especially when under stress and pressure. The little things by themselves aren't usually sexy or glorious. The fact of the matter is that we gain confidence from doing the little things well. The little things, the basic fundamentals, are what set us up for success and, for sure, not doing them well can lead to failure. We can't practice them enough. My experience is that doing the little things well sets us apart from others. A diamond ring is a little thing, but it makes a big difference. As a symbol of beauty, it sets a woman apart. A diamond is formed under pressure. Discipline, under pressure, sets us apart and makes a big difference in our lives and the lives of those around us.

We have a system at my office where we put digital tabs on pages of legal documents to identify issues that still need to be negotiated. If we get lazy about using that little tab, we might miss an issue that could cost our client millions of dollars. That little tab can be the difference between a job done poorly and a job done beautifully, especially under times of great pressure and stress. Often, we have multiple deals closing at the same time involving hundreds of documents and thousands of pages. Can you imagine the nightmare of having to remember all the issues in that many documents? I created the tabbing system so I could sleep at night and so that we could do twice as many deals as most others. During a string of closings, I had an opposing counsel ask me, "How do you guys keep up with it all? How do you not miss anything?" The tabbing system allows me the peace of mind to leave work at work and to have beautiful times with my family and friends and to explore other interests and adventures without worrying about work.

Recently a lawyer friend of mine and I were lamenting over the lack of discipline in many young lawyers to turn work in on time. He tells his young associates, "If your client has to ask, then it is late." What he is really saying is: Be disciplined to communicate with your client about the status of your assignment. Clients hate late. They love on time and early. If you communicate then you are almost always early or on time. Do clients want to hear excuses and explanations, how busy we are, how stressed we have been? No. Typically, they don't care. They want what they want when they want it.

My wife and I hired a contractor to build our home. We hire folks to help us keep it maintained and to fix problems. After years and years of hiring, do you know what the number one thing I use to determine who I will hire? It's a small thing, but it is big to me. Do they communicate with me? Do they promptly return phone calls? I am a busy person. If I can't rely on someone to communicate with me about schedules, then they don't get hired.

Many years ago, my wife and I were invited to join a bunch of friends in Bar Harbor, Maine, for some R&R. On the second or third day we hiked up Beehive. It was more like mountain climbing than hiking. It was dangerous, beautiful, and inspiring. Along with us was a friend who was an army ranger. He taught us that at all times we need to have three points of contact with the mountain—one hand and two feet or two hands and one foot. His advice got us up that mountain. There were so many places that were treacherous, and we needed to know that one little piece of advice to keep us from falling twelve hundred feet. The pressure of the situation caused us to learn and follow that little piece of advice with focus and intensity. It allowed us to go on an adventure that we would have not otherwise been able to complete.

Ask just about anyone who has success, beauty, and adventure in their lives. If you drill down far enough, you will find they have the discipline in their lives to do certain little things well.

Jesus Principle—Be Disciplined to Act on What You Believe

The Bible tells us that even the demons believe there is one God (Jas. 2:19), but it is only those who rely on Christ for salvation who will be saved. There is only a subtle difference between belief and faith, but what a huge difference it makes in terms of salvation. Belief is a subset of faith. Faith requires reliance; belief does not. Belief says, "That chair will hold me up." Faith sits in it.

Scripture also says, "Faith without works is dead" (Jas. 2:20 NKJV). Sounds harsh, but faith that does not result in action has no value (i.e., it is dead). Many folks say, "I believe in a higher power," but they can't describe what that higher power does or how it engages with humanity. In my mind that kind of faith/belief is worthless.

So, the fact of the matter is:

If we believe that God, through Jesus, has taken away all guilt, then by faith don't be moved by guilt.

If we believe that God, through Jesus, has destroyed all barriers between us and Him and we have complete access to Him, then by faith go ahead and jump into His lap and say, "Hi Daddy!" and enjoy His company.

If we believe that God, through Jesus, has given us a gift of righteousness, then by faith act as though we are righteous, giving thanks to the one who made us righteous; and when we sin, acknowledge we did not act in accord with our new character.

If we believe that God, through Jesus, has forgiven us from all wrong—past, present, and future—then by faith don't hold on to regret and shame and likewise forgive others. Don't wait until you feel ready. God has made you ready.

If we believe that God, through Jesus ... then by faith ... You get the point. There are many other riches in Jesus that need to be explored and lived out.

Just as discipline in football and life leads to success, beauty, and adventure, discipline to act on what we believe and acting by faith leads to peace, joy, freedom, beauty, and adventure—the life that God intended us to have.

EIGHT
TRUST THE PROCESS

Football Principle—Trust the Process—Play Possum

When I think of trusting the process, I think about the possum. That's right, the possum. Why? Because the possum instinctively knows that its predators must go through a process to kill and eat. The predator must first identify the target, then chase, then kill, and then finally eat. But the possum interrupts the process of the predator by playing dead instead of running away. The predator's process is broken because there is no chase, and because there is no chase, then the predator can't get to the next step in the process. The possum trusts so much in the predator's process, he bets his life on it. He lays still pretending to be dead under the hot breath of his killer.

Think about the people who are leading you. Have you learned, embraced, and chosen to believe in their process, or have you prematurely judged and stopped trying? Have you embraced your coach's practice plan so that you will give it your all believing that it will bring you and your team one step closer to the goal, or do you just show up at practice and merely endure the process and do enough to get by? Have you embraced the process of watching film, studying the opponent's tendencies, and adjusting your approach? Do you make humble suggestions to improve the process? Remember, it's not where you are that counts; it's where you are headed. If we embrace and trust in the process put in place by our authority, our coach, then we are headed in the right direction and good results will occur. If we don't trust the process, then we have no direction.

An NFL player once told me to make sure my players did at least twenty minutes of footwork every practice. It was an arduous process, but the players bought into it and trusted the process. I believe those drills were the single most important physical factor in the success of our season. The fact is that when we trust in the process, we are training not only our bodies and minds but also our hearts. The heart that can trust in a process to achieve a goal is a healthy heart that will take us to places we can't imagine. Trust in the process set before you and get the most out of it. All the great and lasting coaches and players have a process designed for success.

Life Principle—Live in the Present and Celebrate the Process, Not Just the Outcome

Wishful thinking is only human. It's dreamy and it shifts us into a world of hope and excitement. I remember as a kid thinking (and sometimes saying), "I wish they had a pill for this." Usually "this" was something like getting skinnier just before football season so I could run the ball, building up muscles, getting smarter, and so on. I would often say before a long trip, "I wish Scotty could just beam me there like in *Star Trek*." Okay, I admit, I still think that way and say those things. I know they can't happen, but I still wish, mostly when I don't like the process involved to get what I want. While I love the Bahamas, I don't necessarily like the expense and time and confusion involved in getting there. And when I have eaten too much, I don't really like the process of refusing the next few bowls of ice cream and bags of Doritos.

But the hard truth is that the process is necessary to get what we wish for, whether we like it or not. There are a few exceptions. Someone generally wins the lottery each month. But not me; I have to work. Wouldn't it be cool if we could enjoy the process of getting what we want, rather than trudging through the process to reach some grand goal? How do we learn to enjoy the process? We all want an A in our toughest class, but how do we learn to enjoy the process of doing all the homework to get that A? We all want to win on Friday night, but how do we learn to enjoy the countless hours of drills on and off the practice field?

My kids and my wife enjoy putting together puzzles. I will also jump in on occasion. What makes a puzzle fun? On the surface, it's nothing more than an arduous process of picking through seemingly countless pieces to reach a picture that you've already seen on the box cover. Some of our puzzles have been up to eighteen hundred pieces. What is the mindset that makes the process fun? For me, and probably most people, the process is fun and exciting because we celebrate each puzzle piece that is found. "I found another one!" For others, it could be the mere act of exploration that is fun. "I need one with a straight edge and with purple on the side—here it is!"

Is there a lesson in the puzzle process that could help us in our quest to enjoy the process in other contexts? I think so. Some time ago, my family and some acquaintances hiked to a waterfall in Sapphire Valley, North Carolina. Even though the waterfall was the grand goal, the process was exciting because we celebrated the intermediate steps. We applauded and encouraged each other at each big turn, at building rock stepping-stones across a small creek, at navigating a difficult patch of terrain, and at the beauty we noticed along the way. The hiking group also got to know each other better through exploring each other's interests, backgrounds, and dreams. This lesson can be applied to even the most mundane activities. Celebrate the smaller steps.

There is one big problem in our analogy, though. What if someone threw away half the puzzle pieces and just for fun added some others that didn't fit our puzzle? We would quickly discover that the process was no longer trustworthy. At this point, we quit. What is the use? There is no way to reach our grand goal of a complete puzzle. The puzzle goes in the trash.

While the loss of trust in our mixed-up puzzle is merited, I see a loss of trust happen prematurely in many other contexts. Maybe the better phrase is "lack of trust." Regardless of how we phrase it, when we don't trust a process, then there is no heart and therefore no effort and we feel as though we are wasting our time.

If you ever have the opportunity to lead people in any endeavor, then you will no doubt put in place a process to get the desired result. You will continue to modify the process over time as you believe necessary to get that win, or that medal, or that A, or that promotion, or that recognition, and so on. If you want to be a really good leader, then you would continue to challenge your process to make sure that those you are leading get better and better. What if those you were leading didn't trust your process? You would not achieve your goal, period.

Have you ever tried to get a group of people to do something that required a team effort and it didn't turn out well? It is a hard thing to do to lead and to create a process that folks will embrace. Those who scuba dive know that the process recommends a buddy system. They also know to swim against the current as they go out so that they can let the current help them on the way back when they are tired. The reason for this process is for safety, as well as optimizing the most enjoyable experience. Just about everything we do, no matter how simple or complex, involves a process—making dinner, putting on louder exhaust pipes, getting to know someone, dating, getting married ... the list goes on. Until my kids understand the process of something, I don't have confidence that they can master that thing.

If we skip steps in the process, we are unlikely to get the desired result. I have known many who skip steps in the process of dating and taking the path toward marriage. Skipping steps in that process leads to mistrust and other issues that must be dealt with later in the relationship. It is much harder to deal with those issues when the heat is on.

Likewise, if we are not getting the desired result, we must examine the process we are using.

Jesus Principle—God Has a Process for Our Life. We Can Trust His Process

Some of us are predisposed to lack trust. The New Testament tells us that Thomas, one of Jesus' disciples, did not believe that Jesus had risen from the dead until he placed his fingers into the wounds from the spikes that hung Jesus on the cross. Consequently, those of us who doubt, who require proof before we will believe, are often called a "Doubting Thomas." Others of us simply believe that no one can do things that we can't do. Or we think that if we can't understand a certain thing, then that thing can't happen. Or we judge the book by its cover and let our premature judgment keep us from trust or belief. Or we simply don't have all the facts and make an ignorant judgment about a person, place, or thing that causes our trust to wane. It is so easy not to trust. But when we don't trust the process, we don't try.

God, our ultimate leader, has put into place a process to make us more like His perfect Son, full of truth, grace, and love. I am not talking about making us into a person who can curse trees, walk on water, and turn water into wine. Rather, the Bible says that Jesus was dependent on His Father and had perfect communication with Him (John 17:6–8). Jesus' heart was predisposed to His Father because of love. Jesus knew in bad times and good, His Father was to be trusted. There was never a question, even after forty days of no food. Today, Jesus sits at the right hand of the Father with great glory and power. Jesus also abides in the heart of every believer.

Do we trust God's process for us? Or have we ignorantly prejudged or do we just doubt? Have we the faith to say that no matter what comes our way, we will trust? Can we believe that each day He is moving us closer to Him? Because we so believe, can we rejoice in that day, regardless of the circumstances? Do we believe that He is working in us to prepare us for the good works He will place in our path? Do we trust that His intent is not to harm us but to love and care for us, to rescue us and redeem us and to comfort us? Do we believe that His Spirit is giving us the ability to understand and believe how much the Father loves us? Do we believe that He will complete the good work He began in us? It is a restful and adventurous place to be.

Just like the intermittent celebrations of finding a puzzle piece, we can celebrate the process of each day with the Lord, each day that He has made, each time we feel His love, wonder at His creation, and share His grace.

Did you know that there have been millions of people over time who have come to Christ for salvation? And yet, each time, each one is celebrated with angelic songs of joy in heaven (Luke 15:7, 10). Even the God of all creation celebrates each person in His quest to save all of humanity.

Oh, what would it be like if we trusted God's process for us each day and celebrated each piece of the puzzle He puts together in our journey?

NINE
FULL, FREE, AND FEARLESS

Football Principle—The Bottom Line: Play Full Free and Fearless

I've always thought it would be cool to have a collection of photographs of words or pictures that each football team sees as they enter the stadium. Often you see words like: Determination, Commitment, Desire, Execute, Focus, Do Your Job, Believe, or Trust. These words are intended to inspire the team to a higher level of play. In fact, in many cases the players will jump to touch these words as if to symbolize the desire to reach new heights. These words are one last reminder from the coach of what the coach believes sums up the most necessary quality to win. Most often, these words speak to the heart of a player because knowledge without desire is often meaningless. Have you ever thought about what words you would put above the tunnel? Why those words?

I would be tempted to put, "Worry about us, not them," but in the end I would put these words—"Full, Free, and Fearless." To me, these words embody all that a player needs to play his best, to play to greater heights.

I was once told by a successful sports psychologist that the bottom-line best thing we as coaches can do for our players is to figure out a way to set them free. He said those who play free of worry and doubt play to new heights.

Life Principle—Attitude Overcomes Fear

When I was in my mid-twenties, I was a groomsman in a wedding for one of my best friends, Bill. Bill asked me to say a short Bible verse at a specific point during the wedding service. I remember being anxious about saying this verse in front of all the people at the wedding. When it finally came time for me to say it, fear gripped me and I stumbled and stuttered. I was so embarrassed and disappointed that I had not performed well and had taken away from the beauty of the service. It has taken me a long time to shake that one off.

Why did such a simple little situation rock my world so much? I can remember feeling empty, bound by what people might think of me and fearful of not measuring up to the standard I had set for myself. Just the opposite of full, free, and fearless.

It's all in our attitude—the way we perceive the situation.

What if instead of the empty feeling and the fear of messing up, I was full of anticipation and excitement for the opportunity to contribute to the service? What if I was full of gratitude for being selected by my friend to say something at one of the most important events in his life? What if I was just full of love to help my friend and to speak truth to an audience who might need to hear it? What if I simply decided to be fully engaged, fully committed to giving it my all, and to rebel against the fear?

What if instead of being bound by what everyone might think of me, I rested in the fact that what I was saying would help them in some way? What if I focused on serving the audience rather than making them love me? What if I was so secure in who I was that what they thought of me was irrelevant? What if I simply focused on the task at hand and let the result take care of itself? What if I was free from the audience reaction and simply gave it all I had? What about if I just enjoyed the experience rather than caring so much about my performance? Freedom is a powerful thing. Men and women have fought and died for it. No doubt when we play a sport, play by play, we need to throw off the chains that bind us and play free.

What if I had no fear? "No fear"—in the 1990s a few guys made millions of dollars from that phrase. We saw it on bumper stickers, T-shirts, hats, and surfboards. You might even say that the success of these two simple words proves that we all struggle with fear. Most fear is irrational; mine certainly was. Really, what was there to fear in saying a simple Bible verse? Did I really think that the audience in some way controlled my destiny? Attitudes change by making up our minds to look at things differently and then stand on it.

Jesus Principle—Perfect Love Casts Out All Fear

I once read a devotion from the Fellowship of Christian Athletes on overcoming fear involving the King of the Jungle. The male lion recruits the females to hunt for him. The male has dull teeth. He simply stands in front of the prey and roars mightily. The prey, full of fear, runs in the opposite direction toward the awaiting female lions with sharp teeth and agile bodies and to its death. If only the prey would have "run at the roar," it would likely have lived. The Bible says that Satan is like a roaring lion. He seeks to dissuade us from good works by roaring at us to make us run the other way in fear. In actuality, we need to run at the roar with the faith that we are in the palm of God's hand and hidden in Christ. We don't need to walk; we need to run, having no thought for our own life. What if I enthusiastically resisted the fear of speaking at the wedding and ran into the opportunity in faith that I am His and loved no matter what? As we run toward the roar, the fear will diminish and be replaced by excitement and strength.

What if I view myself as victorious for making the effort rather than being fearful of the result? I am just going to let that one sink in. Try it and see.

The Bible says, "Perfect love drives out fear" (1 John 4:18, NIV). Is there any love more perfect than God's love? He is love. Have we examined our faith to see if we have really received that perfect love in all cases? Have we felt His love in situations that would normally scare us? Our emotions don't lie. If we feel what we know to be irrational fear, then let us take a moment or more to receive God's perfect and unconditional love that depends not one bit on our performance, but rather simply on the magnificent endless love of the One who loved us so much that He was willing to allow His Son to be killed in order to bring us to Him.

Since your mind cannot stand an unanswered question, have you tried each day to ask God, "How much do You love me?" I have been amazed at the answers I receive each day. Count on His love and let it drive out all fear.

Jesus came and offers His life to us so that we will not fear. Fear is something that results from the thinking that we will be punished in some way. Jesus took all the punishment, once and for all; there is no more sacrifice for sin. All that is now left for those who believe is loving discipline. This discipline may at times feel like punishment, but in the end, God uses it to bring us closer to Him. If discipline is what it takes to get closer to Him, isn't that what we really want?

When the captain of a sinking boat called in "Mayday" to shore, some German radio operators responded. The captain quickly exclaimed, "We are sinking!" to which the German operators responded, "What are you sinking about?" ("thinking" in a German accent).

We need to think full, free, and fearless in Christ and feel it deeply.

TEN

CALM THE WATERS OF YOUR MIND

Football Principle—Get Rid of the Clutter in Your Head; Calm Your Mind

"What were you thinking?!" I wish I had a nickel for every time I heard or said or thought that phrase. That phrase is usually said in the context of some mistake that was made. Like when a cornerback gives up an easy touchdown because of a blown coverage or the quarterback steps under guard rather than under center at the beginning of a play. We wonder what they were thinking or if they were thinking at all. The popularity of that phrase reveals a wider truth—that most all of us know that a cluttered mind leads to unwanted results.

I was watching Roger Federer, one of the most successful tennis players of all time, play in a tournament. One of the announcers quoted Roger as once having said, "The calm mind always wins." Wow, I don't think I would have thought of that. I would likely have put more than a few things above a "calm mind" on the list of things that contribute to winning.

For the second year of our football program, we were most teams' pick for their homecoming game, if you know what I mean. One particular game late in the season was against the division leader, and yes, it was the team's homecoming. That team had smoked just about everyone by large margins and looked great on film. We showed up late because of traffic. The other team had twice, maybe three times, as many players and coaches as our team did. All of the players looked the same—big, strong, athletic—and they all had the same uniforms on for warm-ups. Believe it or not, that wave of maroon shirts was pretty intimidating. We had to change clothes between the buses, and we only had fifteen minutes for warm-up because of the festivities. It was a real struggle to keep a calm mind. I began to make excuses for losing the game we were about to play. They were too good, they looked better, they ... You can imagine all that I was telling myself in that moment. We didn't get to warm up, our players weren't focused, we looked like a rag-tag bunch, my players seemed to be more interested in watching the homecoming, we didn't really have a second string or enough coaches to really help, and we did not appear nearly as athletic or together.

"Go to war with what you got." I learned that from one of the NFL players I used to coach with. We didn't have many players, and not many of the ones we did have were very experienced. It was difficult to shake the thought that we were so small in number and lacking in experience. But, around game time, I began to rest in the thought that we were going to war with what we got. It doesn't help me to wish I had more. That is simply a wasted thought born out of fear and totally out of my control. Thanks, Coach, for teaching me to be free with the thought to go to war with what I have and not to waste time wanting more. Somehow, though we trailed most of the game, we were able to keep it close before coming back in the last few minutes and winning in double overtime.

I learned something that night. I can't predict the outcome of a game, and it made no sense to focus on things outside of my control. It made a lot more sense to focus on the things I do know and use that to all of my ability to win and at all times be thankful for the opportunity to compete hard. I learned that my players had a much better outlook than I did. They at least enjoyed the festivities, while I worried about why there was no way for us to win. Their minds were not cluttered;

mine was. When it came time to flip the switch to play with all our hearts, they were ready. I was hanging on for dear life.

I learned that I needed to change my thinking, or rather focus my thinking, and get rid of the clutter.

When you show up to compete, there may be a host of reasons why you won't compete well. I remember one game we showed up to a field that used lights run by generators. Two of those lights had been located right behind our bench. It was unusually loud and the exhaust was horrible. I could barely scream loud enough to get the plays in. About halfway into the game I noticed that out of the ten or twelve generators surrounding the field, only the two generators behind our bench had been positioned so that the exhaust was facing the field—toward our players and coaches rather than away. We need to learn to put aside any thoughts that distract us and use what we do know and control to win.

There are probably many definitions of a calm mind, but here is one I like. A calm mind is a peaceful, unburdened, and focused mind. It is a confident soul. A calm mind can be felt deep in the soul. It is a prepared and disciplined mind that does not allow itself to focus on external things, things it can't control. A calm mind says, "I will play my game; I can do this; I will do this." When your mind is calm, you are able to focus in a way that the game slows down. To the receiver, the ball seems to move through air more slowly; to the QB, the defense moves in slow motion enabling much better reads. A calm mind comes from intense, relaxed focus.

Life Principle—Focus on What You Can Control and Don't Sweat the Other Stuff

I envy those people who can relax and even enjoy themselves and others despite the stress around them. I am such a problem-solver. I tend to sweat everything, including matters outside my control. I am not talking about folks who seem to just dismiss the importance of the desired outcome and who just sort of give up and don't even make an effort to take care of the things they do control.

My daughter seems to have a great balance in this area. Even in the most stressful situations, she is able to slow down, listen intently to and enjoy others, and get rid of anxiety about the unknown. Her attitude seems to be to live in the moment, enjoy it as a gift, and don't worry about what can't be controlled. At the same time, she is a doer. She can get things done. Her head is not cluttered by fear or anxiety about the task at hand. Sometimes her level of peace is unnerving to me because it seems as though she doesn't care. And maybe that is right; she doesn't care—about the things she can't control.

Jesus Principle—God Is Really the One in Control; in Him We Reach a New Level of Calm

God is in control and He has given me an opportunity to compete for a reason. That reason will always bring glory to Him whether it is a win or a loss. In my book, God having glory is a win any day.

You may have heard the story about Gideon in Hebrew history. He and his army were about to fight a bigger and stronger army, and the Lord twice reduced Gideon's numbers. Just before battle, Gideon had three hundred men. His foe had thousands. Gideon had faith, went into battle, and God won. I would have complained to God more than a little bit. God went before Gideon and his army. That is a calming thought.

God is in control of outcomes. We can't increase our numbers or our strength or athleticism just prior to the competition. But we can block out those things we don't control and have a calm mind. We can go deep within ourselves and draw on everything we do know. We can rebel against the lies that pop into our head. We can slow ourselves down and be fundamentally sound, fluid, and balanced. We can find peace in being thankful for what God has given and for the opportunity to compete.

I'm sure we can all agree that a calm mind gives us a much better chance of winning than a distracted one. When you are "in the zone," your mind is calm. My son describes a calm mind as the mindset he has when he is not talking or distracted and he is about to bite into a great meal.

May God grant you a peaceful and calm mind in the midst of the stormy distractions. Strive for a calm mind—one that understands what really matters and can trust God's purposes. One that calms and nourishes your soul. Know that, win or lose, you are in the palm of His hand. Jesus calmed the stormy sea. Focusing on how amazing He is brings peace. He can certainly calm our minds.

ELEVEN
RIGHT PLACE, RIGHT TIME

Football Principle—Right Place, Right Time

I can't remember the exact percentage, but I was amazed at how high it was. It was at least seventy percent—the percentage of plays that don't work simply because one or more of our guys are not lined up right. Does that mean that the play has a much better chance of being successful if we do line up right? Yes, the math is plain and simple.

Then, during the play, depending on your position on the team, there is always an ideal place you need to be. For example, if you are a cornerback, then, if the defensive call is zone coverage, there is a place (a zone) you run to if the QB is passing. If the call is man coverage, then you have a specific place to be in relation to the receiver before the ball is snapped and as he is running down the field.

In football, every player plays his "position." Why do they call it a "position"? Someone's position typically describes a location they line up at, such as cornerback, halfback, linebacker, wide receiver, or tight end. But the complete answer involves so much more. The answer involves not just where you line up but also what you do during the play, depending on the coach's call. Being in the right place during the play puts you in position to make the big play. Many of us have been caught out of position and it feels lonely and horrible, especially if it costs our team. Most offensive plays or defensive plays are designed to trick us into being in the wrong position after the play starts. That is why the coach talks about discipline all the time. He doesn't want you to be tricked into being out of position, out of the play. He wants you to be in the right place to make the play.

Life Principle—Try to Make Sure You Stay in Good Places

Jacob was certainly in the perfect position during what turned out to be a pivotal play in our bowl game. He played inside linebacker in our standard 4-4 defense. His job was to line up in the C gap four yards deep with eyes on the QB. We played zone pass defense. His job was to take two steps toward the C gap at the snap with eyes in the backfield and, if the QB dropped back to pass, then to sprint to his zone. Being a smart, disciplined player, he played it perfectly most of the time. On that particular play in the bowl game, he sprinted to his spot and was able to make a miraculous one-handed interception and then take the ball into the end zone to complete the Pick Six. In my mind, that play sealed the game for us. I still have the picture in my mind of Jacob running into the corner of the end zone for the score. Jacob was in the right place at the right time and that catch was truly miraculous. He was in position to make the big play, and he did so with only one hand. His teammates were inspired and we never looked back.

Being in the right place at the right time applies to all of life. Unfortunately for Jacob, his family and friends, and all those who love him, Jacob was in the wrong place at the wrong time one weeknight about two years after he graduated. Apparently, he had received a phone call to meet someone across town late in the evening. When he arrived, a fight ensued and Jacob was shot and killed. Jacob probably knew his decision to go to that meeting was wrong, but he surely didn't count on his being in the wrong place to be so costly. Jacob surely blessed us in his lifetime. If we learn from his mistake and ask ourselves, "Is this the right place and the right time for me?" then Jacob will bless us in his death and perhaps will save our life.

Asking if we are in the right place at the right time is a great filter for decision-making. We can't control everything that is going to happen, but we certainly can understand the risks. I heard a story of a couple of teenage girls who went to a party where folks were doing drugs. The girls weren't doing drugs, but when a few guys showed up with guns, the girls were caught in the crossfire and killed. Were they in the right place at the right time? Did they know who was throwing the party? Did they calculate the risks? Did they ask, "Is this the right place for us to be?"

While we can't always know we are in the right place at the right time, we can still at least make it a habit of asking the question. Is this the place for me? Does it reflect who I am?

Jesus Principle—Jesus Puts Us in the Right Place with God

As Christians, one of the things we can know for sure, one hundred percent of the time, is that we are in the right place with God. The gospel tells us that based solely on the work of Jesus, if we receive and believe in the name of Jesus by faith, then we are forever in Christ, in the family of God. No one can pluck us from His hand. In an uncertain world that fact is reassuring, and it has many wonderful blessings connected to it. Blessings that are sufficient for all of our needs.

When you are asking yourself, "Am I in the right place at the right time?" don't forget to remind yourself and thank Jesus that you are in the right place with God. If you have accepted Jesus as your Savior, then Jesus makes you right with God. Nothing you can do will change that.

Sometimes it is difficult to identify what causes longings in our heart. Why do I have that feeling there is something more, something else that I need to satisfy me, to make me happy? I think just about all of us can identify with those longings. That's because the One who made us created those longings. I have found in my life that the longing is really a desire to be right with God, to have peace with Him, to be accepted by Him, and to be completely reconciled to Him. For me, those long-ings are satisfied when I remind myself that Jesus has put me and keeps me in right standing with God. He has put me in the right place for all time.

TWELVE
BELIEVE

Football Principle—View Yourself as a Champion and Then Live Up to It

Coach Weiss does a lot of things well. One of those is helping our players believe they are champions, individually and collectively. He looks past the skinny arms, the lack of speed, and the size, and works hard on the hearts of our players to convince them they are champions on and off the field. "Champions on three!" is a common chant before and after practices and games. He compares all that we do to what a champion would do. "Boys, we are champions. Let's practice like champions and play like champions." Sometimes a player doesn't need a kick in the pants. He just needs to know in some way he is a champion.

No doubt, it is difficult for all of us to look past our shortcomings and how we appear to stack up against other teams and players and to believe we are champions. But when we start to believe we are champions or that we can be and will be champions, then a whole new world opens and we begin to live and work and love differently. We practice differently, we play differently, we are better teammates, we work harder, and we care more. It all seems to start with belief.

In my second year of coaching, we needed a fullback. We didn't have anyone who fit the traditional look or attitude of a fullback—one who is tough as nails, confident, stout and strong, reasonably quick, anxious to hit, and selfless. We had to find one. I picked Ryan. Ryan was reasonably quick but weighed 130 pounds, and I am pretty sure he had never before lifted a weight. He was our kicker. But I believed he had enough heart to play the position. He didn't believe he was fit for fullback. When I told him he was playing fullback, he laughed. When he realized I wasn't kidding, he looked at me like I was an idiot. "Really?" he asked. "No, really? You are kidding, right? What are you thinking?" I told him I believed he could do it and do it well. He shook his head. Fortunately, Ryan trusted me enough and had enough belief in himself to at least try. It wasn't too long into the season that Ryan had learned to block without getting killed by the linebackers, and his favorite play was carrying the ball straight up the middle into the teeth of the defense—that play was called "Yellow 2." He gained a lot of yards for us that season and scored many times. Was it true that Ryan could do it, even though he believed he couldn't? It certainly turned out that way. So maybe we *can* do things we currently think are impossible. It just seems to take a little belief and a little effort. As coaches and teammates, we have to say and do things to create belief.

Life Principle—Can't Never Could

What do we really believe? That question is an interesting one. Have you ever thought about it? The answer to that question is important to who we are. Belief influences how we think about something and consequently our actions and feelings—what we do and whether we are sad, happy, or glad. Belief influences every aspect of our life. It influences who we vote for, how well we follow instructions, who we look up to, how much risk we are willing to take, who our friends are, whether we are honest, whether we give up, who we marry, where we spend our money, how we spend our time, what we are afraid of, and our passions. How often do we think about what we believe? What we believe is the essence of who we are. Do you want to know who you are? Do you want others to understand you and know you? Do you want to make a difference? Then find out what you believe. We question others' beliefs all the time. Have we ever analyzed our own beliefs?

We are defined by our beliefs. We need to test them to see if they are true. I know this—just because I believe something doesn't make it true, and just because I believe something is false, doesn't make it false.

The concept of determining what we believe takes hard work to really understand. To determine what we believe we have to take a closer look at what we say and do and how we feel. Then we have to do the "going deep" work to figure out what belief results in that type of behavior or feeling. Have you ever said or thought before a game, "Look at those guys—we are going to get killed"? That statement is based on a belief that we have the ability to predict the future and that what we see with our eyes and the judgments we make will control the future. We all know that the future is not in our hands and crazy things can happen. So, why not at least believe there is a possibility of playing well and winning? Why not leave room for any possibility? If we don't at least try, then the improbable is never possible.

Once we determine what we believe, how do we change our beliefs so that we live a life worthy of life itself?

Belief is a product of many outside influences and experiences. Our brains pick up pretty quickly on what it takes to survive and what facts and circumstances lead to what results, so we develop fears and doubts about things we don't know and about outcomes that we don't control. Our brain begins to develop thought patterns that tell us we can't do something, that we will be embarrassed if we try, that our dreams are nothing more than a dream, that whatever we do won't make a difference, that we need to live in the real world, and that there is no use in trying. My dad used to say, "Can't never could." My addendum to his saying is that "Can sometimes will." Another addendum, "Maybe I can," is enough to get started.

Jesus Principle—I Am a Champion in Christ No Matter What

To change our beliefs, we must seek the truth—the truth about the past, present, and future.

I was on one national championship team as a young player, and I have coached teams that were certainly recognized for overachieving. It was nice to have the titles and recognition, and it was glorious for a time, but the wins have not convinced me I am a champion. For me personally, working hard, trying my best, stretching my best, and believing against all circumstances makes me feel more like a champion than does a win. Simply deciding to believe in myself seems to be the key—believing that I can and will make that block, that tackle, that throw, that catch.

It is important, however, to draw a line where we can no longer believe in ourselves. We do not hold the future; God does. We cannot grant eternal life; God can. We cannot die on a cross to save mankind, but God did. We cannot grant someone the gift of righteousness, but God can. We are not the beginning of wisdom, but God is. We cannot come to live in the hearts of men, but God can.

When we learn to draw that line and lean on God and trust Him for the things that only He can do, then we take another step in our journey to be a champion. When I began to do so, I realized that I am a champion, regardless of anything else and whatever might happen, because I believe in Jesus and His gift of Himself to me makes me victorious eternally, long after all the failures and shortcomings. Jesus is the ultimate champion who comes to live in us and gives us faith and belief. He is the author and finisher of our faith and belief. He motivates me to seek truth and all the things He was and still is today the greatest man who has ever lived and is, in fact, God Himself. He is the embodiment of truth. He has a lot to say about the past, present, and future. It may be worth checking it out for yourself. When I do so, my thoughts and beliefs are always improved and my feelings and actions follow. I am thankful for that.

Belief, based on truth, will never fail. Search for and find truth and then unwaveringly believe regardless of feelings or what others might say. Over time, that belief will translate into decisions and emotions and provide opportunities to live an adventurous and full life. A champion on and off the field.

THIRTEEN
FIND SOMETHING GOOD

Football Principle—Look for the Best in Others

About six years ago, I went to Jacksonville to meet with my Pop Warner coach. I hadn't seen or talked with him in almost forty years. We had won a national championship at the junior midget level under him and he had many other national titles at various levels. In my mind, he was the consummate youth coach. He was still coaching youth football and baseball when we met. It was his calling and he was good at it.

When I called him to ask if he would meet, I was amazed that not only did he remember me, but he recalled the year I played for him and some of the details of the season and my position on the team.

I asked him if he would bring his playbook for his high school teams. I was still trying to figure out what kind of offense to run. I didn't think our personnel matched the spread or any of the other passing fast-paced offenses, but I was confident he knew how to get first downs and score a lot of points from the pro set and I formations.

We met for breakfast. It was great. He gave me his playbook and went over some details of how to teach the various positions and run the offense and defense. And, of course, we reminisced about our season together and he filled me in on what some of my teammates had done after the season. I used a lot of his stuff and it all worked extremely well. He even was kind enough to make himself available during the season for questions. I really can't thank Coach Wilkins enough.

But it wasn't his playbook or his football knowledge that was the most impactful on me or my coaching. It was something he said as breakfast was winding down. He looked over the table at me and said, "Look, if you dwell on the negatives, you will drive yourself crazy. You must learn to pick out the good things about each player and each coach and dwell on those things, openly and in private. That is the only thing that will keep you sane." I thanked him for that advice, not knowing how valuable it would be.

Just like most folks, I like to win and I hate to lose. I have a strong tendency to dwell on things that will keep us from winning. That tendency can be a good thing, but when it focuses on things I can't control, then it is a very bad thing. It is so easy for me to start thinking about things like our lack of speed, strength, or size, or that our best running back is hurt, and consequently, we are going to get killed. It seemed that each week we faced new and old challenges that in my mind would severely hinder our performance, and result in a loss and embarrassment. I can't tell you how many times Coach Wilkins' words rang in my ears—"Focus on the positive or you will drive yourself crazy."

Likewise, we all have our faults. Every player does and every coach does. I found myself thinking too much about so-and-so's bad attitude or inability to get off the ball. I was not a very good coach when I thought that way. I was continually frustrated and disappointed, and the players, coaches, and others around me could see it. However, when I followed Coach Wilkins' advice with respect to each player, I became a much better coach and a much happier person and conse-quently a better asset to each player and to the team.

We had a kid on our team who was one of the best leaders I have seen. Though he was also the best player on our team, that was not what made him a leader. His athletic ability gave him respect as a player but did not make him a leader. He also seemed to want to win more than any other player. When you are the best player and you want to win the most, it is easy to find fault in others. It would have been easy for him to get frustrated when other players didn't try as hard or the coaches didn't care as much as he did. But I didn't see that in him. He restricted his comments and actions to those that built up the other players and the team as a whole. The players looked forward to hearing what he had to say and so did I. He found a way to look for the good and be challenging at the same time. I know this helped both him and each member of the team and the coaching staff. He practiced, as a teenager, what Coach Wilkins taught me.

Life Principle—Good and Bad Can Be Good

Obviously, if I was smart, and sometimes I am, I would apply what Coach Wilkins taught me in all areas of my life. I am a husband, a father, a son, an employee, a friend, a small group leader, and many other things. In all areas of life, in the people I touch and who touch me, there is both the good and the bad, the positive and the negative. It takes effort to focus on the good. My mom always said, "Find the lemonade in the lemon." Sometimes that is a difficult thing to do, like finding a needle in a haystack. But each time I go on that hunt for the good treasure in someone, I am blessed and I think they are too. Not a bad principle to apply to myself as well.

This principle applies to circumstances, too. Do you remember Eeyore from Winnie the Pooh? There are countless examples of people like Eeyore who pick out the negative in every situation or thing. I have to admit, unless they are super kind or funny, it is difficult to be around those people. In every circumstance, however, there is something good, even if it is just to learn something.

Jesus Principle—Thank You, Lord, for All Things

The end result of all this looking for the good is gratitude. The end result of gratitude is peace and joy.

I believe looking for the good in people and circumstances is not natural. Just like being a thankful person is not natural. I believe we must learn it and practice it just like we have to learn and practice our defensive coverages and offensive blocking techniques. My natural tendency is to dwell on what I don't have, versus looking for the good and being thankful for what I do have. I have more than I think I have.

The Book of Romans says we must renew our mind in order to prove the will of God (Rom. 12:2). Renewing the mind is nothing more than practicing a way of thinking. God also says to give thanks in all things. Praise Him in the bad and the good. This takes practice and faith. Faith that is pleasing to God. When we thank Him in the midst of troubles, we declare faith that He is in control and knows what is best for us and that His intent is not to harm us but to help us.

After making an effort to say thanks in all circumstances, I find myself experiencing more peace with God and His provision for me. I like living thankful. I like looking for the good in things, but it is a battle, and I can't say I don't slip into old thought patterns. What I will say is, the more I practice thankfulness, the easier it is to look for the good and be thankful.

We have been talking mostly about sports, but can you imagine being married to a person who looks mostly at the negatives? Can you imagine being a person who thinks mostly negatively about themselves? Why not try it God's way and look for the good and be thankful? God has so much to say about how much He loves us and how special we are to Him. Isn't that reason enough to look for the good in others and say to God, "Thanks so much for being good in me and to me"?

Once again, maybe Jesus is the key. When God looks at me, He sees the good in me because He sees Jesus. Scripture says my life is "hidden with Christ in God" (Col. 3:3, NIV). Scripture also says I am one hundred percent accepted in Christ. God isn't really trying to change me because He is dissatisfied with who I am. He is, in love, trying to guide me into truth, to the knowledge of His Son, and to bring me closer to Him.

We certainly can't be thankful for people we are just trying to change. We need to love them and accept them and simply guide them to the one who loves them perfectly.

Rather than focusing on the negatives in others, fertilize them with the love of God and watch them grow. Maybe do the same for yourself.

FOURTEEN
DO YOUR JOB

Football Principle—It Really Is Simple—Just Do Your Job

If you listen to any coach long enough, you will hear the phrase, "Do your job!" I have heard that phrase said repeatedly during games by some of the most successful coaches ever. It is not a hard phrase to understand, just three easy words. It simply means that each of the eleven players on the field has a unique job to do. If everyone does their job, then the team has the best chance of success. Sounds simple.

If it is that simple, then why do coaches say it so often? The phrase is far too irritatingly familiar because it is said so much. "Do your job!" "Just do your job!" Those words ring in the ears of many athletes. Why the endless reminder? Do we not understand? Are we not doing our job?

On the surface, we as coaches are simply trying to get each player to do what we have taught them. Every offense, defense, and special team has a specific scheme. Within every scheme there are specific jobs to do. And each job has various methods and techniques. For example, just about every defensive scheme has a player who has to contain a ball carrier from getting around the end and down the sideline. For example, in some defenses that is the defensive end and in others it is the outside linebacker. There may be adjustments from week to week depending on the schemes, players, and tendencies of the next opponent.

On a deeper level, when we say, "Do your job," we as coaches are trying to get each player to play "team" ball. I grew up playing back-yard football. In backyard football there is very little, if any, offensive or defensive scheming. Usually, the scheme is no more than man-to-man on defense. And for offense, we simply draw plays in the sand and then it is every man for himself. We all want to score the touch-down and we all want to make the tackle. We all want the glory. It doesn't work that way in true team football. At least it shouldn't.

In my Pop Warner games, I saw so many offensive linemen simply stand up, turn around, and watch the running back. He usually did not get very far. It frustrated me that these linemen weren't interested in doing their part. Maybe they felt deep down they should be the one running the ball. Maybe they felt that the running back didn't need what they had to offer. Regardless of the reason, the whole team suffered because of it. Backyard football is fun, but it can't accomplish what team ball can accomplish.

In a perfect setting, each player does his assigned job. To do so effec-tively, we must trust others to do their jobs. If we try someone else's job on top of ours, then we are usually rendered ineffective. On top of that, the coach has no way of properly evaluating your performance or the performance of the teammate you don't trust. Sometimes your job might be to help out a teammate, but not until you have done your primary job.

When we do our job, we often give up our glory for the glory of the team—we play team ball. Sometimes doing our job might feel insignifi-cant, but we must trust that there will be times when it will be signifi-cant. The defensive line provides a great example here. As coaches, we stress over and over again the concept of gap defense. Each defensive lineman has a gap and is told to fill the gap and penetrate into the backfield. But the temptation is to simply stand up, engage the offen-sive lineman in front of us, and look for the ball. If the defensive lineman yields to this temptation, then there is a greater probability for a big play for the offense. If he would just trust the job given to him, then he would make far more tackles.

Most of the time, any given scheme is designed so that most of the team on the field is supporting other players. In providing such support, players are playing team ball—doing their job. If we keep this in mind, our team will have the greatest chance of success.

Life Principle—Doing Our Job Is More than a Game

Losses in sports hurt. When the scoreboard doesn't read in our team's favor, it isn't fun. The great thing about sports is there is always another game for the team. However, as an individual on that team, if I don't do my job in the game or in practice, it is likely someone else will get a chance to do the job right. Yes, I will get a chance to show I can do the job in practice, but the coach may lose trust in me and let someone else prove they can do my job in the game. When I get benched, as an individual, it really hurts and sometimes there is no second chance for me no matter how hard I practice.

The same thing is true in life. If we don't do our job for our employer, then we get fired or we remain in the same position for far too long. Either way, it is miserable.

I also have a job to do as a father and as a husband and as a friend, and so on. If I don't do my job, then the team suffers, whether it be a family, a small group, a group of employees, or otherwise.

The tough thing about these real-life jobs is when the job isn't done, there may not be another chance to do it right. Long-term damage can occur if I don't love my wife well or love my kids well. It is important for me to measure my words and actions. For example, a ten-minute outburst of anger can have years of detrimental effect. Is that really what I intend to happen?

My wife and I have this thing we do when one of us doesn't quite do our job well (usually me). We learned it at Kanakuk family camp. We simply ask for a "do-over." When something doesn't come out of my mouth right, or I am harsh or lazy, I ask for a do-over. She grants me grace and I humbly get it right the second time.

The thing is, we know when we need a do-over. We know when we've said or done something and it has left us with the feeling something isn't right. We may feel that we have every right to have said or done what we said or did, and maybe on the scales of short-term justice that is true. But it really isn't about our rights, is it? It is about what's best for the team long term.

When we learn to work together (and it is something that has to be learned over and over again), then we begin to see the power of TEAM. For example, my wife and I do a much better job raising our kids together than when we are on different pages. I can't tell you how many times one of us was fed up to our eyeballs with the actions of one of our kids. In those cases, if we didn't have each other's support, it would have been horrible.

Divorced couples with kids provide another example. It must be difficult to cooperate with someone you now may view as an enemy. From my observation, the ex-husband and ex-wife spend too much time hammering each other. It must take so much emotional energy for each person to be constantly "on guard" and to find ways to degrade the other. The truth is that the two are still a couple (a team) when it comes to the kids. Each person loves the kids. So, I ask, if we love the kids, why do we hammer the one who is also responsible for raising them? How hard is it to get degraded by the ex and then turn around and love the kids? How much easier would it be to love the kids if the parents decided to cooperate and be friends, not just in front of the kids? Here is the tough question: Do I hate my spouse more than I love my kids? What is the job description that gives the team the best chance of success?

On a deeper level, we have only two jobs in life—to give and to receive. As an experiment, take a day and then maybe seven days in a row and think about what you do and think about it in the context of those two jobs. To give means to do for others, whether it be your family, your friends, your employer ... whomever. To receive means to do for yourself and to receive what others have to give.

Jesus Principle—Jesus Did a Great Work and He Continues to Do His Job

You know God did a job and He continues to do His job and He never fails. Do we know what He did and what He continues to do? The Bible says He made a covenant with us. That covenant means He made some promises and that He has His part of the bargain to hold up. Do we trust in that, or do we, as Adam and Eve did, try to be like God and take His role?

Here is the challenge—read scripture and outline the job description that God gave Jesus and then trust that He did what it says He did, that He is doing what He said He would do, and that He will continue to do His job to perfection.

One of my favorite promises from Jesus is that He will complete the good work He began in us (Phil. 1:6). The good work that He began is when He came to live in us. The completion of that work involves living through us and making us more like Him. That means that Christ is continually changing me for the better. I can relax in that truth.

After the cross and the resurrection, Jesus didn't just relax and fold His arms and tell us to take it from there. He remains active. He is doing His job. It is glorious and freeing to trust Him to do His job.

Jesus continues to do for us by grace that which we could never earn.

That is His job.

FIFTEEN
TRY HARD, REGARDLESS

Football Principle—Try Hard Regardless of Circumstances

Circumstances are unpredictable in so many ways. Often, I think one way and the exact opposite happens. We just never know. Sometimes a win feels unlikely, and other times I feel like we should and will win. The presence of certain circumstances and the unpredictability of future circumstances sometimes cause us to lose heart. It is difficult to let go of the circumstances and perform with all of our heart.

There have been so many times when our players showed me the way by playing with all their heart against the odds, against the circumstances. They have helped me put aside my fears and petty feelings based on circumstances and begin to see how we could win in our hearts and minds from the experience and love a challenge regardless of the circumstances.

In my Pop Warner coaching days, the losses hurt so much. Sometimes, late in the game when it was clear we were going to lose, I would whisper to my heart, "I don't care." I thought I was just protecting my heart and no one else could see, until a kid came up to me late in a game and demanded emphatically, "Coach, don't give up on us!!!" They knew. Ouch!

I have seen players who don't care. They come to practice when they feel like it, they give half effort during practice, they barely listen to the coaches, they don't encourage or lead their teammates, and they miss a tackle and act like nothing happened. There is certainly freedom in losing when you really don't care. But what does that attitude do for us and those around us in the long run? The truth is, it gets us in the habit of not caring. And then one day, when it really counts, we have a much tougher time leaning into the hardship even though the game of life is on the line.

Long before starting the football program was even a thought, I was at one of our high school basketball games. I recall one game where we were behind by forty points against a giant of a team. Our boys had fought mightily all game. In fact, with thirty seconds left, they were still diving for loose balls! I was so proud of their effort. And, here is the key—so were they! They cared more about their great effort than they did about the scoreboard. I hope those boys will remember their extra capacity to give effort when, later in life, they feel as though they want to give up on a child, or a wife, or a friend. I hope they will keep diving for loose balls all their life. The important thing is to care enough to try again and again and to always give it our all regardless of the final outcome.

Life Principle—Just Try

Although it sounds simple, trying our best is a difficult thing. Why is it so difficult? What stands in our way? What causes us to react so negatively to the circumstances at hand when the outcome doesn't feel like it will be favorable? Could it be pride, fear of embarrassment, unbelief, fear of not measuring up, lack of commitment, lack of emotional energy, lack of focus, lack of effort, or fear of losing? Whatever it is that holds us back is not really the issue. The issue is identifying the important things to care about and attaching our efforts and goals to those things. In so doing, we will put aside what holds us back.

What I have learned is that the most important matters are the matters of the heart, followed by the mind and then the body. All are important, but it is heart that gives us strength and courage. The mind is important, because what we think shapes the beliefs in our hearts.

Nike says, "Just do it." To me, that phrase implies focus and determination. Two very good things. But if unbelief is what holds you back, then you will likely not even try. Sometimes, we need to hear, "Just try." Just try, with all your heart, enjoy the game, and work for the win. Enjoy the journey. Let go of the possibility of loss or embarrassment and of the temptation not to care. How can we improve unless we try our best? If you are good at not caring, then don't care about the outcome, but do care about effort and enjoyment. Games are so much more fun when we try hard and leave everything on the field. And so are our jobs, our marriages, our relationships, and everything else in life.

Jesus Principle—God Is the One Person Who Is Worthy of Playing for All the Time

Previously I mentioned a Scripture that meant a lot to me and that I wanted to bury deep in the hearts of my players. Colossians 3:23 says, "Whatever you do, work at it with all your heart, as working for the Lord, not for human masters." The fact is that if our work attitude depends on what others might do or think, then we will work in fear. Fear is a strong motivator, but it also stiffens and paralyzes us. Paralysis and stiffness keep us from performing at our highest level. There will be times when I frankly don't like my coach or I am disappointed with him or some of my teammates, or in life, my teacher, my parents, and my boss. It will be tough to play hard, with all my heart, for someone I don't like or someone with whom I am disappointed. The same holds true if I am playing for myself. Sometimes I am not worthy of being played for.

On the contrary, God is always worthy. Based on the quality of His love and His sacrifice for us, there is no reason to be fearful or disappointed. He is always there, always loving us, always ready to bear our burdens, always ready to accept us even in our bad times, always forgiving, always guiding, always caring, and the list could go on and on. He is the coach I can play for with all my heart regardless of the circumstances.

The Bible says that love never ends and that God is love. There will be many times in the game of football when the hope for a win is gone and there will be many times in life when hope is gone. But there will always be love ... there will always be God. Play for love, play as if you are doing so unto God and in His love with all your heart.

SIXTEEN
LEAD

Football Principle—Teams Need Leaders and You Can Be One

When I was growing up, my coaches made a big deal about being a leader. When I started coaching, I made a big deal about being a leader. All coaches want leadership. A team filled with talent but no leadership does not perform as well as it should. A team with mediocre talent but with great leadership seems to beat expectations more often than not.

We have all been on teams that lack leadership. On those teams, it seems like things move slower; there is less heart and a lack of intensity. Players tend to stand around looking for someone to follow. Coaches plead for someone to step up.

It helps if your best players are leaders, but that is not always the case. Sometimes, those who are leaders take the team in the wrong direction. Imagine what would happen if your best player was lazy in practice, cut corners on laps, did drills half-heartedly, talked over the coach, showed favoritism, created cliques on the team, and so on.

A friend of mine went on a mule ride with a large group in the Grand Canyon. On these rides, there is always a lead mule and the rest of the mules follow down the treacherous narrow path. The group was so large, they ran out of follower mules and my friend, unbeknownst to him, received a lead mule. Not only that, they started my friend at the very back of the pack, as far away as possible from the other lead mule at the front. My friend's mule fought to get to the front of the pack, taking every chance to pass another mule and sometimes jumping over thin air to pass another mule. My friend made it out alive, but it was the ride of his life. No doubt his mule threatened his safety and that of the rest of the group. Sometimes players who fight to be the one in front threaten the well-being and success of the team. Frankly, I am not sure I would call those players leaders because they are not serving the best interests of the team.

Typically, when a coach says, "Step up," he is looking for anyone and everyone to lead in matters of intensity, focus, dedication, determination, improvement, desire, attitude, and the like. In other words, things unrelated to skill level. Therefore, each and every one of us can be a leader.

Life Principle—Serve One Another to Be a Great Leader

I rarely use the word "leader" anymore, other than to point to a character quality in someone I want others to emulate or to refer to the highest qualities of the role models in my own life or the great things others have done for me over the years. The word "leader" is an easy term to use but difficult to really understand.

Leadership does not mean being bossy. It does not mean I have the right to tell others what to do. It does not mean that others must follow. A leader does not force others to follow. It does not mean that I have to be vocal or monopolize the conversation. It does not mean that I have to grab the stage. It does not mean that others are obligated to respect or fear me. It does not mean that I deserve notoriety or reverence.

In my experience, a leader is someone who works harder than anyone else, who makes those around them better because of their attitude and work ethic, who is willing to sacrifice for the greater good, who communicates love with their actions, who is not swayed by the fact that others may not agree, who gives without expecting return, and who holds to internal absolutes that bring folks to a higher excellence. Few, if any, have all of these qualities. But even if you have one such quality, then you can be a leader. It doesn't matter how many of these qualities your best friend may have. Show up with what you have to give and give it. This principle applies at home, at work, and in every walk of life.

When I was in college I ran for office. It was a large campus, with over twenty thousand students. It was a lot of ground to cover. There was a girl named Helen I didn't really know well, who unselfishly volunteered to wear a sandwich board around campus. The sandwich board was a political advertisement for me. She spent days walking all over campus wearing that silly sandwich board. She never asked for anything in return. I was so grateful. It was hard for me to believe someone would do that. To me, Helen's actions were the ultimate picture of service. She taught me a quality of leadership at the highest level.

Jesus Principle—The Greatest Servant and Leader of All

It almost seems blasphemous to call Jesus my servant, but if He is not our servant, He is not our God. Jesus served me with His life, His death, His resurrection, and the work He is doing in and through me today. He leads us into the service of others and into leadership. Consider these points of His service to us:

- Christ works hard to complete the good work He began in you when you received Him as your Savior. Christ provides access to the Father. He is our High Priest. He provides forgiveness and leads us into truth. His burden is light because He does the work. He is at work in us to strengthen our soul. He is very busy for each of us.

- For these reasons, Christ makes us better servants of others. When we realize how well Christ serves us, then we become better servants of others. Our life becomes more valuable to others and more fulfilled and satisfied. Christ never misses a beat in His service to us. He does not make excuses nor does He provide explanations for not getting the job done for us. His performance does not depend on our efforts.

- Christ gave His life for us. The sinless for the sinful. The godly for the ungodly. There is no greater sacrifice. When we focus on His sacrifice, we become more willing to sacrifice. In one of our games, our QB came to me at halftime. I had called his number a lot so far, and understandably he was tired. He also knew that I wanted to call his number more but didn't want to exhaust him further or expose him to injury. He said to me, "Coach, don't worry about protecting me or tiring me out. Do what you think is best for the team." I can see Christ standing before the Father saying, "Don't worry about Me. I am willing to do what it takes for those You love."

- The life of Christ demonstrates love. The more fully we understand that love, the more free we are from fear, worry, and anxiety. Christ does not lead with the spirit of fear. I see so many people these days programmed to simply choose the path that is least fearful. What if we chose the path with the most love? That is the path of Christ. That is the path that asks, "What is the best for others?" and indirectly it is the path that leads us to fulfillment. Christ's life demonstrated love because He is love. Christ is at all times fully engaged in pursuing us as the object of His love and doing the will of His Father. The Bible calls us His bride. He pursues His passion for His bride inside the structure of the will of His Father, inside truth. We can do the same thing if we discover our passions and then just live truthfully while pursuing those passions.

- We never see Christ worried about what others think. He came for a purpose—to rescue, redeem, and restore us. He came to seek and save the lost and heal the sick. As He pursued this purpose, He had many detractors and naysayers. Never did they sway Him from His purpose. What is your purpose on your team? What can you best do to accomplish that purpose? If it means running the warm-up lap faster, don't listen when others say to "slow down."

- In pursuing His purpose, Christ had internal absolutes. These absolutes are derived from the will of the Father. These absolutes could not be compromised. There are absolutes in life and everything in it. Things that we would on some level fight for and maybe even die for. On a different level, there are absolutes in football: things that must be done in order for your team to accomplish its purpose. These absolutes are often referred to as fundamentals—hard work, excellence, discipline, determination, alignment, stance, focus, and so forth.

Have you pondered what Christ offers you? Have you pondered His examples of leadership? How can His offerings to you and His examples benefit your team? Even one thing you can do will help. It doesn't have to be big. Christ has a way of taking the small things we do and making them big. He is our ticket to leadership.

SEVENTEEN
ENVISION PERFECTION

Football Principle—See It Before You See It So You Can See It; Envision the Perfect Play

Derric said one of the coolest sayings I have ever heard—"If you don't see it before you see it, then you'll never see it." I had to think about that one for a while. If you don't see it before you see it, then you'll never see it.

Talk to a great artist. They can see in their mind what they want to paint. They see it in their mind's eye before they see it on the canvas. I am amazed at that type of gift.

When I was trying out for baseball pitcher, my dad would tell me to envision the perfect pitch. It helped me throw strikes. One of my football coaches made us lie still and envision the way the game might go. It was very effective to assist our execution.

Whether we are talking about defense, offense, or special teams, envisioning the perfect play will draw us closer to perfection. Practicing what we envision is the natural next step. Envision the way a play is supposed to work and what might happen if it is run perfectly. Work toward that vision. Our team's go-to play is a power run through the 6-

hole. We spend a lot of time envisioning how to run this play perfectly. Start with perfection and keep your eyes on it and don't look away. Don't settle for less than you envision.

Let's make sure we have a vision for how we want the game to go and how we want to perform each play. Each player should have a vision for how he is to perform and the result of each play. With such a vision, practice should have more meaning and purpose.

Life Principle—Envision the Desired Result Before You Begin

A great songwriter hears the note and lyrics in their mind before they ever reach paper. Pro golfers are great at envisioning the shot before they take it. I am told Arnold Palmer envisioned his shot as a robust purple line. Purple was for passion.

Derric said he leaned over to Mrs. Disney at the grand opening of Epcot and said, "It is too bad Walt isn't here to see this." Mrs. Disney said, "Oh, he saw it alright, long before there was ever a shovel in the ground." He saw it before he saw it so he could see it; so that we could see it, too. Millions have benefitted from his vision.

This principle applies not only in sports but also in all areas of life. Most businessmen have a business plan. It seems to logically follow that we would have a vision for what we want our marriage to look like, for what we want our relationship with our kids and friends to look like, and so on. Let's make sure that before we start something, we know where we are headed. This doesn't mean the vision can't change and grow, but if we aim at nothing, we will hit it every time.

Jesus Principle—Envision Jesus as Perfection, and Keep Our Eyes on Him

Scripture says to fix our eyes on Christ. Why? He is perfection in every way. He is the most kind, the most forgiving, the most merciful, the most loving, the most righteous, the most godly, the most humble, the most influential, the most notorious, the most creative, the most powerful, the most worthy, the most giving, the most pleasurable, the most satisfying, the most … the list goes on and on. If we keep our eyes on Him, what do you think happens? If we keep our eyes on ourselves, what do you think happens? How much of our time each day is spent thinking of Him, and how much is spent thinking of ourselves? Do we set our minds on things above or on earthly things?

Scripture also says that without a vision, people perish (Prov. 29:18). Without a vision for our future, without plans, goals, and dreams, and without a foundational guide for our life, we are no more than robots just going through the motions with little to no excitement or hope. We should consider an ideal vision and foundational guide for our work, our marriage, our family, our friendships, and our life. If you had to pick a word or a picture of something to describe each one of those categories, which word or picture would you pick? My wife describes our marriage with the word "hospitality." We love serving and loving on folks in our home.

My overall vision for my life is based on a verse—"See to it that no one fails to obtain the grace of God" (Heb. 12:15 ESV). The thread that runs through most all that I do is to help folks understand grace. His grace rescued me from a mundane, defeated Christian life of duty and obligation, void of love.

In my mind's eye and in my heart, I like to picture myself as a conduit for sharing this grace with folks. I enjoy thinking of ways to communicate grace. It is the vision of Christ, the embodiment of grace that gives me meaning, direction, and thrill.

EIGHTEEN
CHECK WITH THE COACH

Football Principle— Check with the Coach

I knew what had happened. I saw it with my own eyes. Even some of the fans noticed. "He didn't run the right pattern, did he?" many asked. It was close to the end of the game and we had gone ahead of a favored opponent. Then they roared back and now we were in the final seconds marching down the field to regain the lead and win the game. I communicated to the QB for a set of pass patterns on the right side, which had been successful for a long touchdown earlier in the game. But instead of running the assigned pattern, the wide receiver ran one that he thought was better.

Earlier in the season we had some issues with our QB changing the called play. We fixed that problem with some gentle ultimatums and more so with explanations that helped the QB understand the various reasons we call certain plays—usually to keep the momentum going, to keep the defense off balance, and to set up the next few plays or something later in the game. If he changed the play without my permission, it took me and the offense out of rhythm and forced me to start over or recalculate the next move. With more understanding, the QB began to trust the calls.

However, we had not noticed receivers changing patterns without permission. As a result, our last-minute comeback was not successful. The receiver may have been open, but he was not in the place where the QB expected him to be. The QB began to scramble and the play was just ugly. Even if it had worked, I would have still been upset and there would need to be lessons learned.

If a player wants to change something, he needs to check with me or have my prior permission to do so. He can't go rogue and simply do whatever he feels will work without letting me know, no matter how right it seems. I don't even think the QB knew what this receiver was doing. I could understand why the receiver thought the way he did, but the pattern he ran took far too long to get open. The QB looked his way and realized the receiver ran the wrong pattern and started looking for his secondary receiver. By that time, we were doomed.

At practice on Monday following that game, I asked the players to fill in the blank in the following Bible verse: "There is a way that appears to be right, but in the end, it leads to..." There were a lot of blank stares and then the QB spoke up with the right answer—death. "There is a way that appears to be right, but in the end, it leads to death" (Prov. 14:12).

Many of us have hurt ourselves and others with decisions that felt right to us. We have also experienced pain from others' decisions that felt right to them. I asked the players to think about family members who have hurt them thinking they were doing what seemed right to them.

When a player changes the play without checking with me, he destroys the play and potentially the trust of those depending on him. If I were the QB, I would have stopped looking at that receiver at least for a few plays. Not to teach him a lesson, but because I lost trust in him. I need to trust that he will be where he is supposed to be when I need to let go of the ball before I am mauled by large defensive linemen.

The same thing goes for blocking assignments or any other job during a play. No matter whether it is defense or offense or special teams, those around you need to be able to trust you will do your assignment.

Life Principle—Before the Next Move, Check with Someone With Experience You Can Trust

Likewise, the same is true in life. There is a way that seems right to us but will lead to death and destruction. I can't tell you how much money I have lost investing in what seemed right to me but not first checking with someone wiser and then trusting that wisdom.

It seems like success has come to me when I have followed the right process to get there. Success involves steps in the right direction. I need a plan to follow and a strategy and tactics to get where I want to go. Others have helped me determine the steps. Sometimes I have to swallow my pride and ask others to help. I have to ask myself: Based on experience and previous success, do I really know what I am doing? If the answer is no or even maybe, then I need to find someone with more wisdom and experience. When I have the steps right, I feel peace. That receiver had placed his trust not in the play that was called but in the mere hope that all would come together. If we don't have a wise plan and experience on our side, then all we have is hope.

On a number of occasions, my wife and I have been asked to do premarital counseling. Not that we have it all together, but it is so impressive when someone who has never been there before asks for guidance.

One of my bucket-list items is to develop and sell a new product—to create something of value and sell it on the market. I can guarantee you that even if I think of the most awesome product like Velcro or Kleenex or rubber tires, I will be knocking on the door of those with more rounded knowledge on how to protect my product, manufacture it, market it, and sell it.

Jesus Principle—Check with God

Back to the Bible verse—there is a way that seems right to a man but leads to death. Raise your hand if you like the thought of death and destruction in your dreams, your job, your marriage, or anywhere else in your life. Raise your hand if you think you know it all. Raise your hand if you think you know the key to eternal life. The ultimate filter for the decisions we make is the Word of God. The Bible has something to say about virtually everything. If the decision we want to make survives the biblical filter, then, especially in big decisions (i.e., dating, marriage, incurring debt, taking a job), we should confer with those who have more experience and wisdom than us. Learn to check with God in things big and small. He has proven He has our best interests at heart, and His way has proven successful by the test of time. We can trust God.

NINETEEN
VALUE HARD WORK

Football Principle—Excellent Results Are Impossible without Hard Work; Hard Work Must Be Valued

The truth of the matter is that if you are going to be good at football and if your team is going to be a good team, then there will be hard work involved. When we think of hard work, we normally think of sweat, but hard work also involves intense focus and a voracious pursuit of knowledge of the game. Hard work is not the only thing that makes you good, but it is a primary ingredient. Plain and simple, there is no substitute for hard work. I have heard that Alabama's great coach, Bear Bryant, said, "It's not the will to win that matters; it's the will to prepare to win that matters."

There are numerous ways coaches try to get their players to work hard. Obviously, fear is a big motivator, but fear is only effective when the coach is looking. Competition is a good way to bring about hard work. When players compete against each other, they tend to try a little harder. Everyone likes to win and no one likes to lose, but competition has its limitations too. Not everything can be a competition. In the end, it is most helpful if the players believe in their heart that hard work will pay off, and that it will make them better. In other words, it is most helpful if the players believe in their heart and soul that hard work has value.

Hard work has great value. Some never understand this truth. Some choose to believe it and make great strides. Others, like myself, sometimes learn the hard way and see the light only after trying another path.

Just before kickoff, our players gathered in a tight huddle with arms draped over each other's shoulders and screamed a chant reminding them they have worked so hard that when they win it won't be by luck. The players decided to do that chant on their own. It showed me they valued hard work and believed it would make them successful. Who in their right mind would count on luck to win? But that is what we do when we don't perceive that hard work brings value.

Life Principle—What We Value (or Perceive as Valuable) Determines So Much of What We Do, Think, and Feel

Sometimes I wonder why I do what I do and think what I think and feel what I feel. Have you ever wondered why you do certain things? Right now, as I write, I am looking at a beautiful Malibu ski boat docked in my back yard on the lake. Why do I have a boat? Why do I give to charities? Why did we have kids? Why did I go to college and then law school? Why did I marry Jennifer? Why did I work out this morning? Why am I writing this…whatever it is? The questions could go on and on. Everybody has their own list of unending questions they could ask about why they do what they do and make the decisions they make.

Not long ago, I was having coffee with Scott, who has taught me a lot. He reiterated something he said several years back when I called him for advice about a troubled relationship my daughter was having. He said we do what we do because we perceive there is value to us in the doing or in the object of our doing. Such a simple statement, but one that prompted an amazing amount of thought. I began to analyze what I do and the perceived value of my decisions and actions and the object of my affections. Frankly, I had never really thought about it before. I go to work, I coach, and I kiss my wife. I hang with the kids. I eat certain things and certain amounts of things. I watch TV. I play racquetball, and the list goes on.

I began to ask myself, what is the perceived value? And then I began to ask, is the perceived value real value? Or am I just believing erroneously there is value? In my mind, real value is value that begins good and ends well. It has both short-term and long-term value. It does not take one long to find out that there are some things that bring value in the short term, but in the long term, those things lead to undesirable circumstances and complicated situations.

Despite the fact I was convinced my daughter's boyfriend at the time was bad for her (and frankly her for him), my daughter nevertheless thought he hung the moon. Scott explained that, for whatever reason, my daughter perceived extreme value in this boy. He further explained I would not make any headway attacking him. In doing so, I would only make her defensive and further solidify her belief. If I was going to make any headway, then I needed to attack his value to her. Fortunately, the Lord gave me many opportunities to do this, and in a few months, she agreed he was wrong for her. She actually realized he was bad for her. She left him in the dust. Hallelujah!!

Perceived value and real value feel the same, but they can be two different things. When is perceived value not real value? The answer is simple—when it is not based on truth.

Jesus Principle— Find Value in Jesus; Jesus Brings the Greatest Value to Our Soul

When I think about value, I can't help but ask, "What do I value the most?" Generally, we value most whatever brings us the most pleasure, the most satisfaction, and the most security. Sin can temporarily fulfill those needs, but in the end, it will lead to destruction. We need to look at sin as a cheap substitute, with fading negative value. Its purpose is to fill a void in our soul that we have yet to let Christ satisfy. When I am frustrated or disappointed or lonely and seek some sort of immediate pleasure or relief, I need to stop and think, "I have a hole in my heart. Christ, please fill it so nothing else will."

In my experience, the most valuable asset I have is Christ. I don't always act like it, but without Him I know I would be lost and without a deep purpose. With Him, I have contentment, direction, peace, joy, a true friend, and many other gifts. I have what the Bible calls "the riches in Christ." The apostle Peter wrote, "His divine power has granted to us all things that pertain to life and godliness, through the knowledge of him who called us to his own glory and excellence" (2 Pet. 1:3 ESV). It is as if the more we know about Him, the more life and godliness we can experience, regardless of our circumstances. When I find my satisfaction in Him, my pleasure in Him, and my security in Him, then I know that I am in the right place in my heart and mind. And rather than let sin fill those voids leading to destruction, I want to let Christ fill those voids leading to life. Jesus brings the most value short and long term. With Jesus I feel full and content.

TWENTY
PLAY OUR GAME

Football Principle—Play "Your Game"

Last night I played doubles racquetball at the local fitness club. My partner was an excellent player but must have had a bad day. He beat himself up with a thorough tongue-lashing if he hit a bad shot and was visibly and audibly disgusted when I made a mistake. I noticed myself thinking more about him than about the next shot or the next point or enjoying the others on the court or the game. My play began to suffer, which only magnified the issue. It occurred to me that I had a decision to make: Was I going to let his behavior and what he appears to think about himself or me take me out of my game?

All the great coaches frequently say to their teams, "We must play our game." Other coaches express it differently. I heard a great college football coach say, "We need to be more disciplined and consistent." What they are really saying is, "Play the game the way I taught you and don't veer from it. Commit to playing in the manner you have learned and don't let the other team change that. We can't be someone else. We must be who we are and stick to the things we do best."

I have heard it said of Bill Belichick, one of the all-time great football coaches, that his defensive game plan is to take away his opponent's biggest offensive threat. He wants to take the opposing team out of their game.

All great teams are known for something. The Packers under Vince Lombardi ran the Green Bay sweep. It was their bread-and-butter play. Everyone knew they were going to run it and planned to stop it, but most could not. Why not? Because Lombardi spent more time practicing that play than any other team could possibly spend practicing to stop it. If the opposing team did stop it, then it means they were vulnerable somewhere else and Lombardi would find out exactly where. That play defined the Packers. If they didn't run that play, they would not be the Packers. The Packers decided who they were and what their game was. They did not move from who they were and took that path all the way to multiple championships.

The great teams seem to play their game or die trying. They know who they are and they know their brand of football down to the core.

It is super easy to panic if the opposing team is stopping your bread-and-butter play or gashing your base defense. There is a difference between making adjustments and throwing away the playbook. Adjustments are merely derivations of what you already run. They are calculated, anticipated, and logical. On the other hand, you know that you have been taken out of your game when you begin to make up new plays, when you are hoping the play will work without reason, or when, as a player, you change your assignment because what you were supposed to do didn't quite work the first few times.

Life Principle—What Defines Me? Who Am I? Explore the Core

In life, when we know ourselves well, we know what works best for us. We know what makes us unique, our strengths, and our weaknesses. We know what we believe, and we have at least a glimpse of who we are at the core. The core is that place deep down filled with anger, fear, love, darkness, freedom, and/or light. Sometimes the core can be a scary place, and sometimes it can be a place full of light and gratitude. It takes a strong or desperate person to explore the core.

We can mask our core by modifying behavior, but we eventually feel empty in doing so. We can have a beautiful core, with poor execution. The goal is obvious—a beautiful core with good to great execution.

It is easy to get stuck running the same play over and over again with crummy results. When I began coaching, I really didn't know who I was as a coach. I didn't really have a good starting point. The new experience took me out of my game as a person. I tried to emulate other coaches who were successful, but I failed miserably. It wasn't until I found an approach that resonated with my heart that coaching began to pull together for me. I found that approach in a book by Joe Ehrmann, *Coaching Inside Out*. My dating life was a similar story— same old play with not-so-good results. It wasn't until I understood my core and how to satisfy it that my approach changed and I was then able to get married.

As we discover our core, we can establish a game plan that we love for our life. How do we discover our core? There are a number of personality tests that help us understand ourselves and others better. I have studied or taken most of them. The Enneagram seems to have given me the most insight. I recommend *The Road Back to You* to help you understand the Enneagram. Life's circumstances help us understand who we are. Remember that emotions don't lie. The same circumstance in life may bring out love and compassion in one person and resentment and anger in another. The emotions show what is in our core.

Once we gain insight into our core, we find that we can live a more authentic life. If we don't like what we find, we can adjust our beliefs and thinking patterns to move the core to a better place. We are never stuck!

Jesus Principle—A Higher Calling: To Be Defined by Jesus

A series of repeated failures prompted me to explore my core. I found too much emptiness and fear. I found I was wearing a mask. I gave up the mask and challenged God to show me who I was.

The answer was that I am a special person who God loves very much, but I was in need of His Son to give me life, to guide me into truth, and to give me intangibles I could not obtain for myself. I needed to rely on Him to receive and give love. He became my core.

As a Christian, my game is Jesus, and He is love. Loving God and loving others is my life's filter for my decisions and actions.

My brand is Jesus. I am defined by Him. He is my identity. He is the most important person in my life. He is the primary influencer of who I am, what I think, and what I do. I am more grateful for Him than I am for anyone or anything else. By knowing Him, I have **everything** I need for life and godliness. **Everything** is enough for me. He is the vine and I am the branch.

Most of the other influences in my life try to take me out of my game. Indeed, it is a battle. You know what I am talking about—what other people think, and not wanting to disappoint anyone; thinking that money, power, "likes" on Instagram, and physical conquests will bring me lasting happiness, and just the general distractions of life. I am tempted to battle against those things from taking center stage in my life. Frankly, the best thing for me to do is to fix my eyes on my game— Jesus. When I do, the competitors tend to melt away. The greatest thing is that even if the competition is successful in taking me out of my game, Jesus is always there with open arms ready to give me what I want, to fight for me, and guide me in life.

Have you decided what your game is? Who you are and what you are about? Where your happiness comes from and how you want to play the game of life? Read the following poem by one of my best friends, Kennan Burch, and see if you can find what defines him.

The Artist and the Audience
by Kennan Burch

The Artist has given me a ticket to His concert of life; His all-consuming music touches every part of me.

Everything I see, hear, touch, taste, smell, and even comprehend are all part of the music of the Artist.

May I never forget that I am the audience and not the Artist, that I am the receiver and not the giver!

For at times I'm tempted to summon the Artist to recognize me for my song,

And to woo others in the audience to hear me too,

But I find the sound of my song drowns out the music of the Artist.

It is only when I lay down my own instrument and focus toward the stage, that I begin to hear music loud and clear,

> Music so consistent I cannot imagine an Artist with such rhythm

> Music so beautiful I cannot imagine an Artist with such creativity

> Music so vast I cannot comprehend an Artist so big

> Music so complex I cannot imagine an Artist with such intelligence

> Music so intricate I cannot imagine an Artist with such attention to detail

> Music so diverse I cannot imagine an Artist with such diversity

> Music so vibrant I cannot imagine an Artist with such life

> Music so freely given I cannot imagine an Artist with such love

May I never choose to ignore the music of the Artist, or attribute it to mere happenstance, for therein would lie my greatest offense.

It is written that the Artist knit me together in my mother's womb, that He knows when I get up, and when I lie down, and that He counts the very number of hairs on my head.

For an Artist so great, to invite me to His concert, and play His songs for me ... I am honored, I am humbled, and His music is certainly worthy of my attention.

May I not perform good works out of duty, but may I enjoy the music so much that my natural response is the applause of good works.

May my life not be known for the things that I have done,

But for the music I hear, the praise I express, and for encouraging others to listen to the music.

In so doing the Artist will be honored. I'll enjoy the concert, and maybe you might find new meaning behind the music and join in the applause of the Artist.

But the ultimate experience lies not in simply enjoying the music and applauding the Artist; it is found when I lay down my life and become an instrument in the hands of the Artist and He begins to play music through me. That is where I find meaning, purpose, and a heart that comes fully alive.

May we all enjoy the music, applaud the Artist, and become instruments of His music to a world in desperate need of hearing it.

TWENTY-ONE
JUDGE ME FIRST

Football Principle—How Do I Measure Up against My Last Performance?

One season years ago we had a record year for offense and had some miracle plays that were fun to watch. Our QB set rushing and passing records that most likely will never be beaten at our school. In one game he had over four hundred yards in the first half. If you were on offense, it was a good year to keep track of the stats. We struggled on defense, however, and the stats weren't so great. Special teams were acceptable and came through for us on a few occasions. While stats don't determine the outcome of a game, they are helpful measurements of performance.

I enjoy watching individual players keep track of their stats, number of tackles, yards per carry, hurries, interceptions, sacks, highlights, and so forth. The inevitable result of keeping stats is thinking about how you measure up against others. This comparison can be dangerous if it results in pride or discouragement. Comparison is often the thief of joy. However, the most helpful use of stats is to answer the question, "How do I measure up against myself?"

Before I look at the performance of others, I need to look at my own performance. It doesn't matter what others are doing if I can keep the mindset of improving a little each day. I heard that Bear Bryant used to tell his players he only needed a little improvement each day. If I am the fastest one on the team and I focus on how I compare to others, then I may have no reason to improve. But if I judge myself and my own efforts, I will be continually motivated to improve.

Remember my QB that set all the records? He would always run harder than everyone else during practice despite the fact he outpaced his teammates by a wide margin.

Physical stats and measurements are easy to keep. How fast am I in the forty? What is my shuttle time? What is my vertical leap? How much can I squat?

Knowledge stats and measurements are just as important as the physical ones, but more difficult to track without written tests. Do I understand coverages? Can I read defenses? Do I know tendencies? What is everyone's job on a particular play? What is my coach thinking? Why didn't that play work? Why is the linebacker lining up in a different position? What does it mean when that player is in the game? What stance gives me the best chance of success? Why does my coach keep yelling at me to stay low?

Maybe the most important stat of all is the most difficult to keep or measure. More important than the physical stats or the knowledge stats is the attitude of the heart. Will it push through difficult circumstances? Will it help others? Will it be a team player? Is it eager to learn and to follow instruction? Does it build others up or bring them down? Is it determined to succeed? Does it let go of the past and fix its eyes on the goal? Does it learn from disappointment and failure? Does it accept blame? Is it thankful for the game? In my experience, it has more often been the attitude of my heart that has determined the outcome. As a coach and a parent, I feel it is most helpful to coach the attitude of the heart.

Life Principle—Judging and Measuring Myself Is More Important Than Judging and Measuring Others

It is important for me to measure myself in all three categories—body, mind, and heart. Judging myself is the most productive judging I can do. Judging others is the least productive and perhaps destructive to me and others. When I judge and measure myself, it is not for the purpose of condemning myself. We have to be careful with ourselves. Judging myself keeps me balanced in my view of myself and others. It helps me improve in all areas of life including relationships, work, play, and pursuing my dreams. Judging myself helps me empathize with others and is necessary for humility, which is necessary to receive grace. We all want grace.

Jesus Principle—We Have No Standing to Judge Others and to Think Ourselves Better

As a believer in Christ, one of the saddest things for me is when I or my brothers and sisters judge and condemn others. Not only do we have no right to do so, but the Bible says we become guilty of the very thing we judge. When we judge others, it confuses people as to what a Christian really is.

Let me set the record straight. A Christian is someone who has judged his or herself as someone who:

- doesn't measure up to God's glory and is in need of a Savior.
- needs forgiveness from sins.
- needs to cast away regrets and shame.
- is unrighteous and in need of the perfect righteousness required by God.
- doesn't want to be condemned to hell.
- needs unconditional love.
- needs to learn how to love.
- needs unconditional acceptance.
- needs a full and eternal life.
- needs wisdom and truth greater than his or her own.
- wants a strong kinship with others who seem to be on the same journey.

Proper judgment of ourselves leads us directly to Christ.

TWENTY-TWO
WHY COMPETE?

Football Principle—Play to Compete Well

In 2017, most of us witnessed one of the greatest comebacks in Super Bowl history. The New England Patriots, despite having little time left in the game, accomplished what most would have considered impossible. With a pair of touchdowns and two-point conversions, the Patriots tied the game with seconds left to force overtime. Everyone watching that game was shocked. The Atlanta Falcons never got the ball in overtime as the Patriots took the overtime kickoff and then marched down the field for a touchdown to win the game. In the postgame speech, their head coach, Bill Belichick, was asked how they did it. In his response, he mentioned more than several times that they just kept competing. It was clear he had his team programmed to compete regardless of how bleak the outcome might seem.

If our goal is to compete at all times, then we play differently when it looks as though we don't have a chance to win. The converse is also true. We play differently when it is clear we will win the game.

Playing primarily to compete well, regardless of the score, is an entirely different mindset. Over the years I have heard many coaches get really frustrated at their teams for not playing hard when the game is out of reach, in any direction. Just take a look at Nick Saban on the sidelines of an Alabama game and you will see what I mean.

I find it somewhat satisfying to chastise my team at halftime for not competing well, despite the fact the scoreboard is already heavily in our favor. How hard we play should not be determined by how good the other team is or how lopsided the score might be in any direction.

So why is it that Bill Belichick, Nick Saban, and many other great coaches place such an emphasis on competing? I believe it is because they know that the mindset that loves competition is the mindset that will persevere to get better at all times. It is a mindset that will not fold in the face of a loss. It is a mindset that will seek improvement even if the outcome of the game is not a win. They also know that many things in the game of football are well beyond their control and all they can ask is for their players to compete well.

The word "compete" means to engage in a contest for a reward. The prefix "com-" means "with." The basic idea of competition was to solve a problem. The problem was that one could only improve so much by practicing by himself. So, the original purpose of competition was to play with someone for the purpose of getting better. It wasn't viewed as playing against or for bragging rights. It was to get better. Sure, the object was to win, but winning was merely the means to an end. The end goal was to get better. The end goal was to realize potential. Can anything be more satisfying than giving our all to reach our potential —including participating in challenges that may result in defeat?

Whether up or down or playing in a tight game, playing to compete well increases focus, intensity, and perseverance—three key ingredients to improvement. What more could a coach ask for than one who joyfully competes 110 percent at all times regardless of the circumstances? If we want to improve, then there simply is no substitute for playing as hard as we can against a better opponent. I have to admit that sometimes I look forward to games where we are heavily favored, but too many of those games are boring because they are not conducive to success—reaching our potential and being the best we can be.

Life Principle—Make a Goal and Compete with It

The ebb and flow of confidence in life is reality. I wish I could be confident all the time. But that is not the case. My confidence wanes when I am not in control of a situation or life presents me with disappointments and challenges. There are plenty of those, some of my own doing, and some that just seem to come my way.

I have found that making a goal can help me improve and to get through life's challenges. The goal is my competition. Will it beat me or will I beat it? I can use that goal to help me play life better, no matter the context.

Recently, a virus attacked our entire planet—COVID-19. It pretty much shut down the world. We were confined to our homes. The stock market was way down and folks weren't working. It became an easy recipe for stress and loss of hope. However, at the beginning of the crisis, my daughter asked how I was going to use the extra time. It was a perfect question, so I made a goal. I then competed with the goal to read some books and finish writing this one. It helped me navigate through the COVID-19 challenge.

Goals can be intangible too. My wife's dad recently passed away. In my heart I set a goal to go the extra mile by being more sensitive and helpful, and getting the kids to do the same. It helped us through this difficult time and we are better for it.

Challenges pass, but while they exist, if you make a goal, then the challenge can be a great teacher and a productive time.

Jesus Principle—Fight the Good Fight

God's Word teaches us to face trials in our life with joy because the trial teaches perseverance and steadfastness in our faith (Jas. 1:2–3). The full effect of perseverance and steadfastness in our faith is perfection and completion, a realization of greater faith and strength.

Competition and trials each produce much the same thing. Competition requires us to make an effort to be the best we can be. In the same way, trials in our lifetime are an opportunity to persevere in our faith (standing fast based on the promises of God regardless of how we feel or how things may look). Such perseverance produces a faith that will stand up to the ups and downs of life and results in greater faith and a stronger soul.

So many of us define winning in life by the number of material possessions we end up with, but for every time we think we have won, there is someone else who has done it better. The real purpose of life is to be able to say at the end of our lives, "I have fought the good fight [I have competed well] by keeping the faith" (2 Tim. 4:7). So, instead of focusing my life on beating the guy next door or some other measure of performance, I focus on competing well at all times—by keeping the faith that stands on the promises of God and accepting trials as an opportunity to trust and grow.

Greater faith produces a grateful soul. My favorite way to live.

TWENTY-THREE
PATIENT IMPROVEMENT

Football Principle—Patience Allows Long-Term Improvement

At the postseason meeting, I asked Nick if he wished he had one more year to play. Nick had been a serious basketball player his entire athletic life. He timidly came out for football in his junior year. For a rookie, he played well, but the game was so new to him, he didn't have the confidence to play like he did on the basketball court. In his junior year, he played defensive back, but wouldn't play receiver because of the hazards involved with going over the middle. He was afraid and wasn't sure if he would do well. It took a lot of encouragement, but Nick agreed to play football again during his senior year. He almost didn't play. We were counting on him to play receiver his senior year. He agreed but wasn't sure about it.

Nick worked hard and was patient with himself. He didn't give up and stayed with it. Nick's improvement was absolutely amazing. By the end of the season, he was making miracle catches and helping to coach the younger receivers. It was an amazing difference from one season to the next. Needless to say, Nick exclaimed, "Coach, I so wish I had another year to play!" Just think what Nick would have missed if he hadn't played his senior year.

I see so many players who either give up too soon or feel defeated or frustrated or simply don't enjoy the game as much as they want to because they don't feel competent as a player. Others are unsure if they will be any good and don't want to be embarrassed. Recently, I asked a student to come out for spring football. He replied, "I won't be any good." I can remember not wanting to go out for baseball or basketball because I didn't really understand the game and wasn't sure if I could perform.

Here are the laws of improvement—it takes effort, it takes time, and sometimes it is going to be uncomfortable. It takes patience with ourselves and our circumstances. There are no quick fixes or miracle pills for significant improvement. Think about the times your game has improved. Most likely it has involved stress on your game, either from playing someone better than you or a good coach stressing your game in practice by working you harder and faster or making you uncomfortable in a game-type situation. It took time and patience. For those of us who have given effort and time and patiently fought through the discomfort believing that one day we would be competent, we know the riches of improvement—confidence and thrilling experiences and opportunities. Nick is just one of many examples. He patiently worked on his game and was rewarded for it.

Life Principle—Be Patient with Your Baby Steps to Improvement

When I began practicing law, my boss gave me an amazing truth. He said, "If I make the practice of law hard [with extra time and effort] the first three years, then the practice will thereafter always be easy. And if I make it easy [with normal effort and time] then the practice of law will always be hard." Frankly, although I had a lot of respect for his authority, I didn't believe him. I learned the hard way, and in my sixth year, I decided to give extra time and effort for three years with the hope of making the remainder of my career easier and more enjoyable. I knew it would take a lot of patience to make a three-year commitment, and sometimes the improvement was not evident. However, my boss was right, and now that I look back, three years wasn't that long at all. During that three-year period, I had to keep reminding myself to be patient with my improvement. Baby steps.

My friend Jeff gave me a book called *The Talent Code* that he thought would help my coaching. It is about how talent develops. The general thesis of the book is that there are very few naturally gifted people; real talent comes from effort and time. The more intense the effort and the longer the time, the greater the talent development. Time requires patience. The book explained the physiological side of learning. Each time we repeat something, a sheath of myelin develops as a coating on the nerves we are using. The more myelin, the faster the nerve works, resulting in greater physical and mental performance. Each sheath of myelin is extremely thin. It takes many sheaths to make the impulse fly, to make the nerve impulse and ultimately the physical result quick and automatic and decisive. I read that Einstein's brain had the average number of neurons but twice as much myelin. When I learned this, I rested in the fact that however small, effort never goes unrewarded. I also realized that if I could make the effort more intense, then there was a greater chance of myelin development over the same nerves I needed to enhance performance. The bottom line is I became more patient with myself and with others and more confident that if I kept trying, I would eventually get there and so could my players. Thank you, Jeff.

In an effort to encourage me, someone once told me, "It isn't where you are; it is where you are headed." I guess I could have taken that two ways, but I chose to let it set me free from having to be something right now. It allowed me to focus on my goal and not beat myself up for not being there already. I can remember so many times committing to start working out and being so impatient to see results. I can remember working out so hard that I made myself miserable and became discouraged and quit. I needed to be patient and try to enjoy the workout and trust the outcome over time.

The point is this—whatever our goal is, we need to give extra time and intense effort and at the same time be patient with our improvement over the long haul. The same holds true of the folks with whom we are working. I can't disrespect our team for not being great. I need to be patient and think more in terms of whether we are headed toward our greatest potential. Pursuing that path is true success.

Jesus Principle—God Is Patient with Me and He Is at Work in Me

I am thankful God is patient with my improvement. In 1 Corinthians 13, Paul describes love as patient and kind. Since God is love, then He is patient with me. He is kind to me. He promises to guide me into all truth and to complete the good work He began in me. Ephesians 2:8–9 says that God works in me to bring me to the place He wants me to be. He is patiently and kindly working in me to improve me spiritually. If God is patient and kind to me, then don't I owe it to myself to be patient and kind to me?

Perhaps like Nick, you aren't sure about pursuing football or some other goal you would like to accomplish, because it feels as though improvement won't occur at all or quickly enough. Or maybe you have convinced yourself prematurely that you can't do something. Perhaps, like I was, you are struggling with whether or not you are a good Christian and whether you are doing everything you can for God. In either situation, the answer involves time, effort, and patience. In the spiritual realm, it is time focusing on God rather than myself, receiving His efforts to complete me, and the patience that results from trusting in Him. In the physical and mental realm, it involves time at practice, intense effort, and patience that results from the realization and belief that I will improve if I keep trying. Our greatest potential will happen; it simply takes time and effort. Are you willing to give the time and make the effort? The Book of Proverbs says to consider the ant. Considering its size, it does great things, a little bit at a time, with diligent, focused effort. The ant is pretty patient. What would you like to build, and are you willing to work patiently? Are you patient with God's work in your heart, soul, and mind?

TWENTY-FOUR
GROW IN HEART

Football Principle—Our Heart Is Our Most Valuable Muscle

There is no way around it. Competition requires heart. For those with heart, expending "heart energy" is part of the thrill of competition. That is why sometimes it is difficult to enjoy games against a much lesser opponent. As a coach, I feel most successful if I see my young men grow in heart, learn how to dig deep within, and explore their unknown potential. My dad used to say, "When the going gets tough, the tough get going." It takes heart to be tough. I love to see my players overcome obstacles (usually within themselves) and grow to places they could never have imagined. Whenever I heard one say, "If I can do that, then I can do anything," it would thrill me to no end.

Our school doesn't have a weight room, a track, or a field. We are not the strongest, not even close. But I have noticed that we generally have more heart than the other teams. We play hard, we don't give up no matter what, and we are determined to play well. In a sense, not having the physical facilities has been a blessing, because by default we have to coach the heart.

In our first year, we practiced on a field that I affectionately called the goat ranch. There were no lines, plenty of holes and ant piles, and lots of tall grass and weeds. You can imagine how difficult it is to sync up the QB and the receivers on such a field. One afternoon at practice, my QB was having an exceptionally hard time completing a little hitch route to our wide receiver. Over and over again the ball went high or low, everywhere but where it was supposed to go. My QB's feet were just too jittery and he couldn't get balanced before he threw. I showed him the steps, but because the hitch route requires such a quick throw my QB was rushing his feet. The more we talked about slowing it down, the worse it got.

I finally remembered—train the heart. I went over to him. He was pretty frustrated. He knew what to do; he just couldn't do it. His mind was not the issue. In an effort to train the heart, I didn't mention his feet or his throws or what to do. I mentioned allowing his heart to feel patience, and not to be anxious in his heart about how fast the ball got there. The result was like day and night. Not only were his throws on target, but they got there so much faster than his previous jittery rushed throws. It was amazing.

As a coach or a chaplain, we must continue to speak to the heart. We must encourage it. We must challenge it. I believe more than half the time when something is not going right, there is a heart issue involved. We can all speak to physical performance and identify areas we need to improve, but how many of us have learned to coach the heart?

The best book I have read on this subject is one I mentioned earlier— Joe Erhmann's *Inside Out Coaching*. It is for anyone who believes that the whole person (mostly the heart) is necessary for whole performance.

The advantage of coaching the heart is that it will last a lifetime. We all know that being in football shape physically only lasts as long as the season. Physical prowess is fleeting. The heart has the ability to grow unceasingly and the benefits last forever.

As a player, we can learn to include an examination of our heart, when we examine our performance. Sometimes it's not an extra few pounds on the bench press we need. Sometimes it is a little more patience or kindness to ourselves or to our teammates. Maybe it is a little more determination. Maybe it is a little more care. Maybe we need to have a little more fun and less worry. Maybe we need to be a little more serious.

Life Principle—Look under the Hood and Check Out the Heart

In my sixth year of practicing law, I considered my legal career a failure. Since I don't like to fail, I wanted to know why I was not succeeding. The answer was pretty clear—I had not dug in; I had not determined to succeed. I had not decided in my heart to commit to do the hard stuff. When my heart engaged, it paid off. I actually picked a difficult area of the law to learn. I figured that if I could learn that area, I could do anything in the law. My heart got me through the difficulty of learning, and I made it. Thank God. My confidence grew and I believed I had something of value to give to clients.

Almost all of my struggles in life have been the result of a heart issue. I tend to condemn myself when I don't perform well. I tend to shy away from trying if I don't think I am going to perform well. I can be impatient to get to the finish line rather than going through the necessary process. I can be full of fear of embarrassment and failure. I can even be afraid to lose. The list goes on. All of these are "heart" issues. They invade every area of my life, without exception.

When I am suffering from these heart issues, I so want to solve the problem. I am usually first tempted to evaluate my activities—maybe I should do more of this and less of that. Maybe I should work harder at work or come home earlier. Maybe I should do yoga. Maybe I should get a hobby. Maybe I should pray more. Maybe I should try to be nicer. Maybe I should just quit whatever I think is resulting in whatever discomfort I am feeling. Those things may give temporary relief, but the problem usually is I have not gotten to the root of the issue—the heart of the matter.

I do the same thing in my relationships. For example, in parenting I tend to address problems with physical solutions—grounding, taking the phone away, time-outs, Chinese water torture (just kidding), and so on. But it is only when I take the time to get to the heart of the matter that real change occurs. Physical solutions are temporary, while a change in heart lasts forever. Parenting the heart, while more difficult, is much more rewarding.

The key is to focus on heart issues. I can push out fear with love, impatience with patience, anger with forgiveness, timidity with confidence, error with truth, and slavery with freedom, just to name a few. The heart is where we experience what we believe. It is where we make choices on what to value. It is where the mind creates death or life. From our heart flows the issues of life.

Jesus Principle—He Gives Me Heart

There is a Scripture that says, "Physical training is good, but training for godliness is much better" (1 Tim. 4:8, NLT). Proverbs 2:2 (TPT) says, "train your heart to listen...."

One of God's beautiful gifts to us is that we are not left alone to fix our heart. In fact, when we believe in Him and receive Him by faith, the Spirit of Christ comes to live in us. That Spirit changes our beliefs, changes what we value, and fills our heart with joy, peace, love, kindness, patience, self-control, humility, and grace. With our heart full, our outlook changes.

So now when I experience fear, for example, rather than focusing on physical activities, I focus on what my heart is believing, where its focus is, and the source of its fullness. The Spirit of Christ teaches me to believe the truth that sets me free from fear and anxiety and anger. His truth teaches my soul to rest.

Also, because I have an infinite source living in me, I can give freely to others and experience life in a more fulfilling way. Part of experiencing the correction of heart issues allows me to coach in a loving way the hearts of my players, my kids, my wife, my friends, and anyone else. God no doubt uses them to coach me.

All of me is imperfect, except for one thing—Christ who lives in my heart. He is perfection. Also, His Word says that there is no condemnation for those in Christ. It says He has given me a heart of flesh and not of stone. Knowing that He lives in me and doesn't condemn me has allowed my heart to grow and not to be stunted or permanently discouraged by my shortcomings. Jesus is the fix for all heart issues. He keeps me in the game, even when I want to go to the sideline. He is my safe harbor.

So thankful!!!

TWENTY-FIVE
COMFORT AND CONFIDENCE

Football Principle—Simple = Comfort = Confidence

When I feel like the players are thinking too much and confusing themselves, I ask the following questions: Have you ever noticed birds flying in a V formation? And have you noticed there is usually one line in the V longer than the other? Do you know why that is? Most kids spend a little time thinking and then wager a few guesses. The guesses are always more intelligent than the simple answer, which is simply … there are more birds in the longer line. The point is, at least know the obvious before we complicate things too much. Keep it simple.

Coaches and players don't mean to complicate things, but in an effort to prepare for everything, every possible scenario, we often make things too complicated, especially in light of the limited time we have to perfect what we do. It takes time to deeply learn something.

For the first year of our program, I designed the defense. After studying many different schemes, it seemed to me that a 4-4 suited our team the best and gave us the best chance to stop most of our opponents. I tried to think of every formation and variation an offense could throw at us and how we would defend it. I had special calls for so many things. I had adjustments and then I made adjustments to the adjustments, and so on.

In the end, however, we used about thirty-five percent of what I schemed up. It was just too complicated for me to implement and coach. If it was too complicated for me, then it was definitely too complicated for the players. I learned that players can be frozen by complicated schemes. If they have to think about what they are doing during the game versus just being automatic, then they react slower and sometimes don't react at all because they are confused.

In the second year of our program, I was fortunate enough to have a defensive coordinator who had played defense for Alabama and in the National Football League (NFL). I was surprised that we used the scheme I had drawn up the year before. I was even more surprised that my coordinator further simplified the defense. When I asked him about it, he explained that the most important thing for a defensive player is to play free and aggressive. If they are having to think about schemes and calls and adjustments, then they can't be free; and if they can't be free, then they can't be aggressive. Thank you, Simeon.

Some players can handle complicated schemes. Others can't. When I am deciding player roles, schemes, strategies, coverages, stunts, and so forth, I often ask my players, "Are you more comfortable doing it this way or that way?" I want their input. I want them to play free.

A friend of mine and his wife have spent a lot of time and money to help their autistic child. One interesting treatment came from an eye doctor in New York. This doctor worked with autistic children, professional athletes, and folks in between. His strategy was to use eyeglasses and contacts to make the patient more comfortable and secure. In essence, he sought to normalize deficiencies in how the brain processed information sent to it through the eye. Using some of his techniques, I determined which side my players were most comfortable with receiving and dishing out contact. This technique helped me discover that my left guard should be moved to right guard. When I made the move, he flourished, because he was more comfortable with making the hits from that side of the offense.

When we are comfortable with our roles and assignments, we are able to play our game and to play with freedom and confidence. I am not saying we don't maintain a high level of intensity. Actually, we have more capacity for intensity if we are comfortable and confident with the simplicity of the scheme and our role.

Life Principle—Simplify Our Purpose and Live Confidently in That Purpose

Life is the same way. We can easily make life too complicated. We can jumble things up and try to keep too many balls in the air, have too many commitments, never finish anything, and end up always chasing the wind. In Texas, they describe someone like that as having "all hat and no cattle." I also love the expression, "I feel like I am a mile wide and an inch deep." A life without depth of purpose can be and feel insignificant, always searching for more or the next best thing. A better way is to find out who we are and what our purpose is. Only then do we have an opportunity to find meaning and satisfaction. We use our defined purpose as a filter to learn to say no to things that aren't within that realm of purpose and yes to those things that do. Life gets simple and we live with confidence and peace. We are no longer trying to keep up with anyone or make anyone like us. We are safe and free within the confines of our purpose.

These principles can apply to relationships as well. When you look at what my wife and I do as a couple and how we spend our money and time, you would conclude that we like meeting folks and showing them hospitality. We enjoy having people in our home, even staying overnight and sometimes much longer. My wife is so good at that. We like giving. If I would have been a little smarter and known my wife better before we got married, I could have concluded that our purpose as a couple is to be hospitable and generous. It is good for me to ask myself from time to time: What promise did God make to the world when He put my wife and me together? That question puts my head in the right place.

Jesus Principle—Keep It Simple: Focus on the One and Only

In our Christian walk and relationship with God, we can get stuck in a morass of rules and dos and don'ts and focus on our own perfor- mance, *or* we can fix our eyes on Christ and His character and His work for us and in us and through us to others. We can focus on His power, His righteousness, and His mighty deeds and wonder. Scrip- ture says that we have everything we need for life and godliness through the knowledge of Jesus Christ (2 Pet. 1:3). It is so much easier and more effective to focus on Jesus. When we focus on Jesus, He defines our purpose and we begin to use our unique makeup to love and bless others in a way that only we can do. We, by faith, simply receive His love and blessings and then love and bless others the way He loves and blesses us. Note that in the story of Jesus feeding the five thousand, Jesus multiplied and gave the food to the disciples and *they* fed the five thousand. They handed out what Jesus gave them, nothing more and nothing less. When we focus on Jesus and view Him as our source, we simply give away, in deed and in truth, what He has given us, nothing more and nothing less. He made it simple for us—focus on Him and keep the faith. Simplicity is genius.

TWENTY-SIX
FUN

Football Principle—Have Fun and Enjoy the Game

In our hearts, we all want to win. The question is how much "want to" we have. The "want to" has to show up in practice where it takes so much sacrifice. The "want to" also has to show up in the game. Usually when we speak of "want to," the picture in our mind is one of grit and determination. We need grit and determination.

But are we made to always live with grit and determination? Can we be serious all the time?

In my experience, just before the game, it helps most to remind my players to have fun. My players seem to play better week to week if they set out to have as much fun as they can possibly have.

So, while there is time for grit and determination, there is also time to enjoy. Sometimes the two concepts commingle.

The pro football players with the most longevity are the ones who enjoy the game the most. I heard Coach Tony Dungy say once that Peyton Manning enjoyed every aspect of the game, from film reviews to footwork drills. What a blessing to enjoy every aspect of your work.

Some folks don't have to learn to have fun. Others resist it and have to learn to let go.

Regardless of our tendency toward fun or serious work, enjoying the game is not only important but a critical part of success.

I once heard a professional player say the key to his success was his decision before the game to relax and have fun. For me to relax and have fun, I have to know I am prepared; but the truth is that even if I am not as prepared as I want to be, the decision to relax and have fun always calms my nerves, creates excitement, and allows me to play better.

If my goal is to have fun, then my overall perspective on the game is better. It allows all aspects of the game to come together. Sometimes, the individual aspects of the game can hinder my performance. When I focus on my grip in racquetball during the match, my game suffers and it is frustrating. The time to focus on the individual aspects is during practice. Game time is fun time.

Life Principle—Have Fun and Enjoy Life

One of the reasons I love coaching so much is that there is so much in sports that is analogous to life. I want to help my players live better, learn what I and others have learned about life, and avoid the mistakes I have made.

Just as in sports, we must learn to enjoy life, to enjoy ourselves, and to enjoy others. I have to admit in my younger days I was prone to always think I needed to improve and achieve, to view others as a resource and their responses to my performance as an affirmation for my life. I was inclined to think harder work was the answer to whatever emptiness I was feeling and to view God as a hard master who needed to be pleased. The future and not the present occupied most of my thoughts. As you might imagine, there wasn't much room for enjoyment unless I felt I had earned it.

If you don't know how to enjoy life, then talk with some folks who do. Pick folks you admire and ask them why and how they seem to enjoy life so much.

Jesus Principle—Enjoy Jesus and All of His Creation

As I grew in the knowledge of Christ, I discovered that He accepts me where I am with no requirement to improve, that He improved me by providing a way of forgiveness for my shortcomings and granting me as a free gift a righteousness that satisfies His requirements. He put in me His Spirit to guide me and to continue to work within me to better me for the good works that He places in my path. I learned that God is pleased with His Son in whom my life is hidden and that God is not a hard master but a loving, patient, and kind Father who has gone to great lengths to love me and who views me as special. These gifts from God are not the result of my efforts but the result of a loving, caring God. These are things I can relax in knowing that they depend on God and not on me.

Therefore, do I still want to be a better lawyer, coach, dad, husband, employer, employee, friend, and son? Do I still work hard and practice the disciplines of each role? Yes. Now, though, as opposed to my younger days, I can relax in the goodness of God and His continuing work within me. I can enjoy myself, others, and God. I have some good news to give folks I meet—good news that is more effective than the constant striving for self-improvement and success. The daily disciplines are better done from a perspective of love rather than fear.

Just like I remind my players before each game, each day I should remind myself to relax in the goodness of God and rejoice in the day. I can look to His creation as His playground for me, His theatre for me, His continuous reminders of His almighty goodness. I can look at others as His gifts to me. It doesn't mean there aren't ups and downs, but I have found life to be so much better when I seek to enjoy Jesus and all of His creation.

One of my favorite persons in the Bible is David—who killed the giant, saved Israel, and became king. After studying the psalms David wrote, I would venture to say that David would not necessarily want to be known for the heroic things he had done, but for His heart for the Lord. In Psalm 27, David indicated the desire of his heart is to gaze upon the beauty of the Lord and live in the house of the Lord forever. He wanted to enjoy God and His presence.

May we have the same heart's desire.

TWENTY-SEVEN
MY PART

Football Principle—How Can I Bring the Greatest Value to My Team?

When I was a kid, I wanted to be Bart Starr, a famous quarterback for the world-champion Green Bay Packers. I loved the way he threw the ball. He was and has remained one of my heroes. I still dream of being an NFL quarterback, but the only way I could get there at my age would be to buy a team (which would require resources I don't possess at the current time) and have them put me in punt formation late in the game and wing it from there. As time has gone by, I have realized that not enough of me was uniquely designed to be an NFL quarterback.

I started coaching in Pop Warner. While I had a lot of love for the kids and a zeal for coaching, I didn't feel I was doing a good job. Looking back at that time, I realize the problem was that I didn't know who I was. The Bible calls it "desire without knowledge" (Prov. 19:2). I didn't have a style, an approach, or an anchor for my soul. I had no place from which my coaching came. I tried to emulate those who were successful around me, but I wasn't very good at being them. My approach to coaching seemed to change daily. I was a foot trying to be a hand one day and a heart the next. It was no fun not being grounded, and I felt like a ship with no rudder, blown about by my circumstances. I can only imagine how hard it was for the team and the other coaches to follow me.

It wasn't until I found an approach that resonated with my heart and Scripture that I wanted to leave in the hearts of my players that I was able to find "my" approach and then hone my skills as a coach. The point is, if we are trying to "do our job" the way someone else does theirs, it may be helpful, but in the end, for maximum success, we need to own our job. It needs to resonate in our souls and hearts, and it needs to be fully us. If raising my voice on a continuous basis is not me, then why do it? If running a certain offense doesn't fit my team, then why do it? If trying to intimidate the other team with pregame antics is not me, then why do it? If I weigh only a hundred pounds, why should my first choice be to play offensive line? Am I more offensive-minded or defensive-minded (does it give me more pleasure to make a touchdown or stop one from happening)? To succeed, we must keep in mind who we are and our unique set of talents, skills, and internal makeup.

Life Principle—When Looking for a Job, Find Something That Suits Who You Are and How You Have Been Made

I have had the privilege of leading a team at my law firm for quite some time. We have a fair number of employees and partners in my group who have been there for a long time. Unfortunately, though, I have had to fire a few people. I hate it, but if it is in the best interest of the employee, I know in my heart it is the right thing to do. I have been fired from other jobs, and as I look back, I am so grateful for it.

In my group, there aren't many reasons why one might be fired. We give a lot of grace and help and support, but if you still can't do the job, then we have to move on. More often than not, it becomes clear that the person just doesn't have the skill set or the heart to do what we do. Either way, it is not in their or our best interest to keep banging our heads against a wall.

To do what we do at the law firm, you have to be extremely organized, detailed, and skilled at critical thinking and problem-solving. You have to do well under pressure. Some folks aren't wired that way, and even though they have heart they will never get there. We had a young lawyer who was smart and got along well with everyone, but when we gave him assignments, his answers were always wrong. We worked with him for a while on his approach and process to solving problems, doing research, and drafting contracts, but it became apparent this was not the job for him. When we finally parted ways, I communicated to him that he was no less of a person and needed to find a job that could use the skills he had. He did have skills and for as long as he worked in our group, those skills were being wasted because we didn't need them. No doubt someone else did.

It is a good idea to study our skills, who we are, the gifts we have, and our passions so that we can work and serve in a place and an environment where we bring value. Feedback from our parents, other family members, and close friends is always helpful in helping us determine who we are and our skill set.

Jesus Principle—The Glory of God Is Making Man Fully Alive. We Come Fully Alive When We Use Our Unique Gifts to Love Others

We each have unique gifts, and if we use them to love others then we become fully alive. The Bible is clear on this. It says that we are uniquely designed, that God knit me in my mother's womb, that God has a plan for my life, and that He has given me unique gifts to love others in a unique way and ultimately for the glory of God. Some of us are designed to be dreamers, some doers, some preachers, some merciful, some prophetic, some wise, some encouraging, some leaders, and so on. What can be more glorious than to be part of God's plan, to do our job, and use our unique design inside that plan? His plan for us is to receive from Him all that He has to offer and then say thanks and give to others what we have been given. We are each uniquely designed by God to fit into a specific role in His plan. Can the hand be a good foot? Can the heart be a good brain? Our uniqueness is valuable, and it is most valuable when we use it to love others. Praise the Lord for not making us all the same.

TWENTY-EIGHT
SELFISHLY UNSELFISH

Football Principle—There Is No "I" in "Team"

When I talk to recruiters, I have noticed that they intentionally look for unselfish character. A few months ago, I was talking to an agent who was attending an NCAA golf match. This particular agent worked for a national agency that has represented and still represents some of the greatest golfers of all time and their families. He explained how they evaluate players. The deciding factor is their character—their integrity, how well they get along with others, how likable they are, and so forth. I was amazed that he would be willing to move a great golfer off his list based on character. He explained that most of the top kids have the shots and the mental game, but not all have good character.

Why are agents focusing on character? I believe if an agent wants to make someone a star, then they need a client who can work with others. No man can do it alone. This is especially true in team sports. Football relies on teamwork. Teamwork doesn't work if one of the members puts himself or herself above the team. We all want the glory, but if we are so set on getting the glory, then our team suffers and then we suffer. Players who are selfishly demanding, confrontational, and all about their own stats and performance and notoriety are cancer to the team and will eventually destroy it. They get traded to another team that thinks the skills are worth the disease. Bad decision.

College recruiters look at character too. They know the truth now—that bad characters make bad teammates. What is the best thing a high school coach can do? If you ask me, it is to build character. We do these kids a disservice if we don't teach them the right way to be a good teammate. One of the coaches I used to work with would say to the players, "If you are all wrapped up in yourself, it is a pretty small package."

It is okay to be selfish "through our team." Put the team first so that all of its members will be recognized. Our sacrifice for the team is really our best chance to get what we really want—team success and all the rewards that come from that success. Unselfishly selfish—I know what I want, and I am smart enough to know that the best way to get it is to sacrifice for the team's success.

Life Principle—Get Ahead by Serving

When I started my practice, I was told that the best way to get rich is to make other people rich. Do I view myself as a resource for others? Or do I view others as a resource for me? There is a time and place for both, but by and large, what has worked for me is to view myself as a resource to my family, friends, coworkers, and clients. It is the attitude of a servant that benefits me the most. I am tempted sometimes to use others to get what I want, but what has worked best for me is to let others use me to get what they want. It makes sense. When others use me to get what they want, they begin to rely on me. When they begin to rely on me and trust that I have their best interests at heart, I become valuable to them. In business, that value translates into compensation to me and my firm. In regard to my family and friends, that value translates into meaningful, healthy relationships.

Jesus Principle—Jesus Laid Down His Life, and Now Is the Most Glorified

One of the most interesting statements I have ever heard is "the last will be first" (Matt. 19:30). The Bible is full of these types of statements that seem counterintuitive and paradoxical. Though they don't make sense literally, they do in practice. There are countless examples of revered and respected men and women who put others above themselves and became superstars.

Therefore, if we want to be first (selfish) we need to make ourselves last (unselfish). God takes care of the rest and life is full. Scripture says, "But seek first his kingdom and his righteousness, and all these things will be given to you as well" (Matt. 6:33). The kingdom of God involves love and sacrifice. Love and sacrifice make a great teammate, a great boss, a great employee, a great friend, a great dad, and a great husband.

The ultimate sacrifice is to lay down our life. It is rare and amazing that one would lay down his life for a friend or a family member. It is even more rare and amazing that one would lay down his life for an ideology or for people they don't even know. That is what soldiers do. It is most amazing that one would lay down his life voluntarily for his enemies. That is what Jesus did.

And He is now forever glorified. He made Himself last, and now He is first, the Most High.

TWENTY-NINE
PLAY TO SUCCEED

Football Principle—Would You Rather Win or Succeed?

Do not be confused with all the talk about effort and playing to compete. We should also play to come out on top! We play every play to end up with more points than the other team. We make every decision with the goal of winning. We game plan to win. We train to win. We recruit to win. We do our dead-level best to win.

However, we don't dwell on the scoreboard while we are playing or practicing. Rather, we dwell on playing well, reaching our potential, learning the game, developing our skills, putting in maximum effort, and competing. We think about doing our job. We sear our hearts with the belief that we can win. We enjoy the game. We play *our* game. We leave the scoreboard to take care of itself. If we do so, then we can succeed regardless of the outcome on the scoreboard.

If you are into football (or any competitive sport), you have observed the following:

- A highly ranked team after a win with their heads hung low because a far inferior team just gave them the game of their life.

- A far inferior team feeling victorious in a loss because they scared the pants off of a much more superior team.
- A team thinking they had the game in hand, only to lose their winning effort and find themselves on the wrong end of the scoreboard at the end of the game.
- A game resulting in a tie with one team feeling victorious and the other dejected.
- A team make an amazing comeback against all odds with seemingly the "hand of God" on their side.
- The outcome of a game determined by unreviewable bad calls.
- The outcome of a game heavily influenced by weather, player sickness, or injury.

What does all this tell us? Winning can be thrilling and glorifying, but in a certain way so can losing. Winning can be discouraging and disappointing. Winning and losing can be determined by circumstances beyond our control.

Since football is a game, then it is meant to be played to win. However, the purpose of playing to win is to make our best better. Winning is generally far more enjoyable than losing, but the glory of the scoreboard fades over time. In over fifteen years of coaching, I only remember one score, and that is only because I use it for the combination on the lock at our property where we ride dirt bikes.

If success is based solely on the outcome on the scoreboard, then we will end up extremely disappointed even if we have played to our potential and many other great things have happened. And even if the scoreboard has been friendly to us, when our abilities and accolades begin to wane as we grow older, we will feel an emptiness that cannot be satisfied because we are no longer able to be on top. If success is based on the scoreboard, then over half the teams each season are unsuccessful. If success is based on national championships, then all but one are unsuccessful. Win or lose, we need to make such an effort that we are satisfied that your best has gotten better. Define success so that we can succeed regardless of the scoreboard.

The scoreboard is one source of feedback. It does not determine true success. It does not define our team. Success is much larger than winning.

Life Principle—Whose Scoreboard Am I Looking at and What Am I Using It For?

Each culture and subculture seems to have its own "go-to" scoreboard. Usually, it is some sort of objective measurement—dollars in the bank, number of "likes," and number of "followers." I am amazed at us running around asking everyone to "like me." If we aren't careful, that "go to" scoreboard can define us. It can control our self-worth. If it does, then that scoreboard is what we live for—a potentially dangerous place to be. In most cases, there are many things that influence the scoreboard that are beyond our control.

My law firm has goals for me, including number of hours worked and billed and dollars collected, all of which are necessary to run a business. If I am going to work there, I need to make every effort to meet those goals. In a sense, these goals are my scoreboard. However, when I focus solely on the scoreboard and let it determine whether I am successful, then I feel like I am on a rollercoaster of success and failure. Regardless of my effort, I sometimes don't meet my daily goal. I must not let that scoreboard determine whether I am successful. I must include in the definition of success more than numbers on a feedback report. I must include: Did I give my best? Did my best get better? Did I help someone? Did I learn something? Did I enjoy those I work with and the clients I serve? Did I work out of love or out of fear? When I acknowledge that success is greater than just the scoreboard, only then can I be successful when I don't reach my numbers, even though I have made every effort to do so.

In my law firm, my executive committee sets the scoreboard for me. I have to trust them to do their job. But in other areas of life, I have a choice as to what scoreboard to look at. It is not only important for me not to let mere numbers (the scoreboard) determine success, but to also choose the scoreboard that I do look at. Why am I spending so much time trying to get "likes"? Why am I spending so much time trying to put dollars in the bank? Why am I spending so much money to get noticed?

I have a choice as to whether I use my culture's "go-to" scoreboard to define me. Basing my self-worth on a set of numbers (whether I win or lose) will eventually destroy my soul. I need to choose the right scoreboard and even then, only use it as a measure of feedback, while defining success and who I am according to things with true meaning, including service to others, gratitude, effort, pursuing dreams, caring, and love.

Jesus Principle—Pursuing Jesus Can Not Be Measured by a Scoreboard

Playing to win and living to be successful are of course better than playing to lose and living to fail. Is there any greater success than pursuing Christ—pursuing the one whose grace, truth, mercy, forgiveness, and love cannot be defined by any set of numbers? Jesus has no scoreboard. He doesn't count our sins against us. He doesn't stay with the ninety-nine sheep and leave the one who is lost. He doesn't measure our works by how big they are. He doesn't run around trying to be "liked." He doesn't count His followers. He doesn't compare what we have done to what others have done. He isn't blown around by the winds of our culture's "go to" scoreboard. He is bigger than all of that. Our job in pursuing Him is simply to find out how big He really is. The bigger He is to us, the more successful we are. May I find my worth in the pursuit of the one who is bigger than all of life's menial scoreboards.

There is no glory from any earthly scoreboard that can compare to the glory of God.

It seems that all human glory is temporary. Can you believe there are some young kids who play basketball who don't know who Michael Jordan is? The pursuit of the glory of the scoreboard is short-lived and shortsighted.

There is one glory that is everlasting. That glory is the glory of God. That glory has been evident from the beginning of time and will never fade.

Seeking, experiencing, and responding to the glory of God is one of our highest callings. It produces everlasting joy. It is one of the few privileges available to only human beings. He is our only hope of true glory, of everlasting success.

THIRTY
IN SHAPE

Football Principle—Better Shape = Better Football

When the strength coach or the speed coach or the endurance coach says, "One more," they know that strength, speed, and endurance are all necessary to do our best. They know that we need to be pushed to be in the best shape we can be to play football. Although I enjoy action, my general tendency is to be at rest. But I know that playing football and other sports requires a commitment to work out hard and to do so over a long period of time.

When I was a kid I would only work out (doing push-ups and jogging and maybe pumping some iron) about a month or two before the season. I thought this was all that it took. As I look back, I wish I would have started working sooner. The first few weeks of practice were brutal for me because I really wasn't in good shape. I believe that I would have performed much better during the season if I had focused for a longer period of time on building strength, speed, and quickness.

I am impressed with coaches who require a yearlong commitment to being in shape for football. I am impressed with the players who give themselves to working in the offseason to be all they can be.

To play football we must be in shape. The more we dedicate ourselves to being in shape, the better we will play, the more fun we will have, and the injuries will be less frequent and less severe.

Life Principle—What "Shape" Does Life Require?

Let's face it. Ninety-nine percent of the population could be in better shape. Round is a shape but not "in shape."

We need to be in good shape not only physically, but also mentally and spiritually in order to face the rigors of life and to better enjoy the good times.

I once heard a great measure of being in shape—how quickly do our muscles recover? In other words, when we burden our muscles to the limit, how quickly can we perform again? An athlete who can run like a cheetah down the field only once every ten minutes is not much good for the team. We need that athlete to be able to perform over and over again with only minimal interludes of rest.

One of the best athletes I have coached would sometimes try to take himself out of the game in the first quarter. I would just smile and say no. I knew that he could stay in the game even though his body was telling him something else. He was an amazing physical specimen, but he was not in great shape for football. We had not pushed him hard enough in practice. We corrected that.

We can also tire mentally, emotionally, and spiritually, based on overwhelming facts and circumstances and the rigors of daily responsibilities. If we learn to exercise our minds, stretch our emotions, and dig as if for treasure for spiritual truth, then we won't have to take ourselves out of the game to recover before reentering life.

Let us not forget to find ways to exercise mentally, emotionally, and spiritually. We need something to stretch us to improve and to be in better shape. For me, the practice of law (and in particular, solving problems) stretches me daily intellectually and emotionally. Also, being involved in the lives of my family and others stretches me emotionally and spiritually. Sometimes it is hard work (just like push-ups), but it is very rewarding (again, just like push-ups).

Jesus Principle—How Long Does It Take My Spiritual Muscle to Recover?

From a spiritual standpoint, when I feel empty, anxious, lonely, angry, condemned, fearful, burdened, unlovable, tempted, unforgiven, unliked, out of favor, unpleasing, or unrighteous, how long does it take me to grab on to the truth found in scripture to bring me to a point of peaceful enthusiasm or a place of rest in my soul? If truth sets me free, then error and lies bind me (take me out of the game). When I am bound by error, how long does it take for truth to invade the error and set me free?

When I am weary of life, I am amazed at how long it takes me to come to Jesus, who said, "Come to me all you who are weary and burdened, and I will give you rest ... for I am gentle and humble in heart and you will find rest for your souls" (Matt. 11:28, 30). When circumstances are beyond my control, I am amazed at how long it takes me to come to Jesus and rest in the fact that He is sovereign and has everything under control. When I don't feel that I am doing a very good job managing my life, I am amazed at how long it takes me to say, "Jesus, You live, not me." When I don't measure up to my standard of what I think a Christian ought to be, I am amazed at how long it takes me to realize that I possess Christ in me who is the sole measure of Christianity (apart from Him, I am nothing). When I am tempted, I am amazed at how long I allow the temptation to play with me before seeking His grace, which the Bible says teaches me to say no to sin. When I am tempted to think I am something, I am amazed at how long it takes me to be humbled by my shortcomings and His overwhelming greatness.

Jesus is always the key. He is the way, the truth, and the life (John 14:6). Coming to Him sooner rather than later means we are in spiritual shape. If we can renew our minds to think truth rather than worldly thoughts, then we are much better equipped to be loved and to love others, and to truly experience the "riches in Christ," referred to so many times in scripture.

THIRTY-ONE
HYDRATE

Football Principle—Hydrate Regularly and Stay in the Game

In our second spring game, we took the field with twelve players, ten of whom played both ways. The twelfth had never played football before. I had thoughts of barely being able to complete the game dancing around in my head. Sometime around the beginning of the fourth quarter, our tailback began to cramp in the larger muscles in his legs. I had to let him rest. Cramps in the larger muscles can be dangerous. My remaining player went in to play tailback, but of course, our offense was at a third of its potential because not only did we not have our best runner, but we also lost our blocker on pass plays. That remaining player also substituted for the tailback on defense. What should have been a decisive win for us ended with the opposing team stalling on our goal line in the last seconds of the game.

Could it be that just a few more sips of water would have allowed the tailback to play the whole game and allow our team to avoid the close call on the goal line at the end of the game?

Proper hydration is one of the more mundane pieces of the puzzle of success in football, but oh, so necessary!

The experts say that proper hydration is a habit, not a last-minute thing the day before or the day of the game. Drinking the proper fluids just before the game is like brushing your teeth four times just before you see your dentist. As hard as we try, we just can't make up for the bad habit of not brushing and flossing on a regular basis.

Proper hydration also involves *not drinking* certain things like coffee and sodas that cause dehydration.

Life Principle—What Well Are We Drinking From?

Whatever we ingest—whether physically, emotionally, mentally, or spiritually—affects who we are and how we behave, how we perform, and how much we enjoy life.

The food I eat and the liquids I drink are key to performing well in the game of life. The extra five pounds above my belt is a distraction and discomfort that I don't need to take with me into life's battles or celebrations.

The same is true for what we put in our minds. Consider the phrase, "garbage in, garbage out." It only makes sense. How can garbage turn into something good in our bodies, mind, or heart? It is true that the lobster eats all the unwanted junk on the bottom of the sea and yet they turn that junk into an amazing delicacy. The same is not true of us. Sometimes I put something in my mind that has a lasting negative effect. It takes a while to push it out and I am reminded that I am not a lobster.

The opposite is also true. Good in, good out. If we want to be the guy who makes a positive lasting difference, then let's ingest and expose ourselves to that which is beneficial for us and others.

I have a friend who says, "If you want something you've never had, then you have to do something you've never done." Maybe it's time to change my intake physically, emotionally, and spiritually.

Jesus Principle—Who Can Satisfy My Soul? Drink the Living Water

The Bible says to renew our minds with His truth—truth about who He is and who we are so that we can prove out His will for us. It also says to guard our hearts, for out of the heart flow the issues of life. We are also to present our bodies as a living sacrifice so that we live for the higher calling. We are also to discipline our bodies to remind us that our bodies are the temple of Christ for those who have received Him.

In the gospel, we are reminded that we must ingest Christ (i.e., by faith we must receive Him into our body, mind, and soul). Jesus said that He is the living water and whoever drinks of Him will not thirst. In 2 Peter 1:3, it says that through the knowledge of Jesus we have everything we need for life and godliness.

Therefore, the question for us becomes, do we properly hydrate on Christ? Do we do so on a regular basis (not just in church or in youth group)? Do we rebel against hydrating on temptations and sinful activities that quench His Spirit within us?

When I was in the eleventh grade, one of my final exams asked the question: If you were stranded on the North Pole and had a bottle of whiskey, should you drink the whiskey to prolong your life? The teacher's point, and mine, was not against alcohol. Rather, it was to recognize that the alcohol in the whiskey is a vasodilator and provides a false sense of warmth and ultimately would lead to freezing to death sooner (with less of a chance of rescue). We ingest things that feel good on a temporary basis, but ultimately lead to destruction. I can have false beliefs and feelings that certain things won't hurt me, even things that provide pleasure.

Remember that Christ is the way, the truth, and the life. If we hydrate on Him, we will not thirst. In other words, we will be satisfied and there will be no need for the imposters.

THIRTY-TWO
DECIDE AND COMMIT

Football Principle—Commit on a Deeper Level

In one of our jamborees, we played two teams that were bigger, better, faster, and more experienced (and probably better coached!). Because of how young our team was, I decided to have only fifteen offensive plays. We worked at perfecting those plays and I was proud of how quickly our players learned and understood the plays. We had only three players returning at the same positions.

I spent a lot of time trying to put players in situations where they might question their role in the play and do something different than I had taught. I wanted them to understand their job and be disciplined to do it each time regardless of what the other team threw at us. There were some adjustments in certain circumstances but very few.

I did all this because I wanted to chip away at and eliminate indecision and confusion. Indecision and confusion are enemies of commitment. Commitment is necessary for execution and success.

We did well in the first game with our execution. Each player did his job and there was full commitment by each player to their roles on each play. It took us ten minutes to score, but we did so with few mistakes. In the second game, their defensive end was giving us fits. Players recognized this and began to shift their thinking and their execution. I could see players moving in different directions, picking different players to block and the runners second guessing how quickly they would hit the hole. My players lost their commitment to our scheme. We let that defensive end take us out of our game. We became indecisive and confused, which slowed us down and left us even more vulnerable—a recipe for frustration and failure.

While maybe we would not have been successful on every play, I believe if we would have committed to what we had been taught we would have done much better. Games like those are helpful in becoming more disciplined to our commitment to our jobs on each play.

Other sports are no different. For example, many pro golfers close their eyes to envision a shot. It is part of the process they go through to fully commit to a shot (e.g., low draw, high fade, etc.), and to get rid of any indecisiveness. The least bit of confusion, the least bit of indecision, or the least bit of lack of belief or trust causes the player to give less than one hundred percent.

Life Principle—Do I Decide Well and Commit to Follow Through?

We must learn to make good decisions and commit to them. Confusion, indecision, and lack of commitment rob our freedom, joy, and ability to get things done and accomplish our goals.

I regret that too many of my decisions over my lifetime have not been well thought out, have not been tested through conversation with wise folks, and have been fueled by impatience and blocked by fear.

Good decisions are a product of a good process and a strong filter. It helps me to discuss decisions with my wife and others that I trust, to research the options, and to pray. Does the decision I am about to make help me and others? Does it match up with my passions and talents? Does it cost too much? Can I afford the risk? Does it match up with other long-term goals?

Just making the decision is not enough; I must commit to executing. Sometimes I am distracted by the immediate stresses of life or by another "shiny object." I must learn to set aside those things that compete with the execution of a well-made decision. I know folks who make great decisions and then stall on the 5-yard line because of a lack of commitment. I can be one of them if I'm not careful.

Jesus Principle—Can We Out-Commit Jesus?

In the Bible we read, "A little yeast leavens the whole batch of dough" (1 Cor. 5:6). The context indicates that even a little legalism ruins our attempt to live under the waterfall of the new covenant of grace. I must commit to living under grace. In other words, I must commit to receiving and trusting what God has given me. I must commit to believing that God is one hundred percent committed to me and my well-being. I must commit to looking at scripture as a love letter and not as an arrest warrant. I must commit to believing He loves me and accepts me despite my faulty performance. Only then can I experience that love and then fall in love with Him and live the abundant life. Only then will I have the ability to give that love to others, the love described in 1 Corinthians 13.

Remembering and reminding myself that He is far more committed to me than I will ever be to Him is the key to committing to Him. He never asks me to do anything that He has not already done Himself. He knew that for me to feel safe in trusting Him that He would have to be the initiator and that He would have to love first. He knew that He would have to pave the way. He knew He would have to give me His Spirit to guide me into truth. He knew that He would have to be my advocate and friend.

Thanks be to God that I am not left on my own to live this life. He is one hundred percent committed to me. When I commit to these truths, the purpose of my life is clear. Indecision and confusion melt away. Life is much more manageable, and the outcomes are more rewarding in a committed relationship with the Almighty God.

THIRTY-THREE
HIGH-LEVEL CONSISTENCY

Football Principle—Consistency Can Take Us to a Higher Level

My nephew, who plays golf, took the lead in the first round of a tournament that would have taken him to the sectional qualifier for the U.S. Open. However, he played less than his potential in the second round and missed the qualification. Later at another tournament, he shot a 65 in his first round to take the lead in a thirty-six-hole qualifier tournament for the U.S. Amateur championship. Then on the second day, he played consistently enough to remain in first place and qualify for the U.S. Amateur.

My favorite college football team once had a kicker who could kick the laces off of the ball. He made a 75-yard field goal in practice. Almost every kickoff goes out of the back of the end zone and sometimes through the uprights. We know he can do it, so the only question is, can he do it consistently? While we dream and aim for perfection, the real question is, can we be consistently really good?

Can we consistently make that block, make the throw, make the catch, make the kick, make the hold, or whatever it is we need to do?

There are few things in sports rewarded more than consistent performance at a high level. Momentary excellence is really cool, but consistent excellence is the real thing.

When I think of achieving consistent excellence, I immediately think of hard work, intense practice, strong competition, and expert guidance. However, in my experience, those things are not enough. Real consistency also requires a consistent inner attitude (what is my consistent daily motivator?) and a vision in my heart of a grand destination (where would I like to end up?). In other words, real consistency is based on motivation and drive toward a desired destination.

Life Principle—Consistent Excellence Is Born and Grows from Motivation and Stimulation

Just like in sports, consistent excellence is highly rewarded in life. Meeting and exceeding your sales quota for the first time, for example, is great, but doing it over and over again is what brings home the bacon. Buying your wife flowers and throwing her a surprise birthday party is an awesome thing, but it is the day-in and day-out love that brings a rich, pure, and impactful marriage.

Just like in sports, consistency arises from two things: (1) an inward motivation and (2) an outward stimulus. How do we find those things?

To find inward motivation, we must find out what makes us tick, and how we are wired. Once we find it, we must embrace it and use it for our benefit. For me, I seem to have an expanded sense of responsibility and achievement. I like to learn. Those things motivate me in all areas of my life. Others have expanded gifts of loyalty and relationships. Some have expanded gifts of maximizing, making things bigger and better. Many have the gifts of dreaming and vision.

To find stimulus, we must think in terms of reward. What is it that I am striving for? What is my ultimate destination? Can I see it and feel it? For example, as I lead my team at work, I picture a well-oiled machine that provides opportunities for care and growth, and at the same time is well-known as a provider of excellent service for our clients. I want to retire knowing that I have helped create something bigger than myself that will continue well. If possible, the stimulus should include both tangible and intangible rewards.

Jesus Principle—Thank God My Relationship with Him Does Not Rely on My Consistency

I recall trying to be a good Christian on a consistent basis. There were times when I felt successful, like when I gave a big amount to the church, or taught a Sunday school lesson, or told someone about Jesus. But I kept getting interrupted by this thing called sin. I fought against the sin but it seemed futile. I was fighting and losing and not living. I viewed God's Word as a measuring stick and was always on an uphill climb. By most folks' standards, I was what some would call a pretty good Christian. What that really meant, though, was that compared to most, I was good at doing the things Christians normally do in our culture.

I viewed God as a sort of policeman. He was sitting up in heaven with His arms crossed hoping I would do well. Deep in my heart, I was not satisfied with my performance as a Christian and I struggled to do better but couldn't find any consistency. I also didn't think God was satisfied with me either. I wanted Him to be proud of me, but I did not feel I was worthy very often. Consequently, I didn't experience peace, contentment, or any other reward in my heart.

Finally, I gave up doing anything that seemed like it was in my own power to be a better Christian. I stopped praying, giving, going to church ... all that type of stuff. I told God that I was tired of playing the game and not getting anywhere. I just wanted joy and peace and to be able to rest in my soul. I told God that if He really lived in me then I needed to experience something only He could do.

It didn't take God long to show me He lived in me. In about a week or so, I developed an insatiable desire to study Romans. I couldn't wait to get up each morning and journal my way through each word.

It was in Romans that I learned for the first time that when I accepted Jesus and received the gift of eternal life, I was also given a number of other free gifts. These other gifts included being deemed righteous because of Jesus. I had been struggling for so long to become righteous on my own. Dang! All that work for nothing. God knew my efforts would be futile, and through Christ, He paved a way for me to satisfy His lofty requirement. Other gifts that I had been striving for and never realized were freely given to me included forever forgiveness, free and full acceptance by God, free and full access to God, all the gifts of the Spirit, free and forever love, and free guidance into truth. I also learned that it is His kindness that teaches me to say no to sin, rather than His might and power.

Wow! In Christ, I can cease striving for the gifts He has given me and simply receive them by faith. Just like salvation and trust, they will never be taken away from me. I finally experienced the unfailing consistency of the true gift-giver. He was my last chance at the Christian life, and He came through and has consistently reminded me of His gifts in my journey. It is much better living out something that I have than it is to work my tail off and never get there.

Amen for that! Thanks be to Christ.

THIRTY-FOUR
SAFE PLACE

Football Principle—The Players Need a Safe Place

When I was in the seventh grade, I got in a fight at school with Paul, whose locker was next to mine. What began as harmless fun—peeking into each other's locker—somehow escalated. Coach Corker picked each of us up by our collars and took us to the principal's office for swats. We knew we were in trouble when Coach's big hands lifted us off the ground. I remember the sting of those swats to this day.

Being in trouble with the coach is not foreign to anyone who has played competitive sports. Whether our troubles arise from missing practice, missing class, mistreating a teammate, not giving maximum effort, not paying attention, not turning in homework, or missing a tackle, we generally know when we are in trouble with the coach. Any good coach will hold us accountable in some way.

Any good coach will also push us to expand our limits. A good coach will not let us rest. How many of you have heard the phrase, "Do it again and do it right!"? We are pushed to do things we would not normally push ourselves to do. In these cases, we may feel as though we are in trouble with the coach because it feels like punishment. In actuality, the coach is simply trying to make us better. I love the scene in the movie *Miracle* where the U.S. Olympic hockey team has just played dismally and the U.S. coach made them skate sprints over and over, all the while stopping only to ask an individual skater whom he plays for. When the players finally figured out that they didn't play for their colleges, and rather played for the U.S., the sprints stopped. What seemed like heavy-duty punishment was really an exercise to achieve team unity and a grand purpose.

As coaches, while we need to hold our players accountable and challenge them, we also need to make sure our players know that we are a safe place for them. They need to know we would never intentionally or recklessly do anything to hurt them. We may sometimes make forceful adjustments to their minds, bodies, and souls, but we would never injure them. They need to know that they can come to us with anything and not be condemned. They need to know they don't need to guard their souls around us. We don't need to be their best friend, but we do need to be someone with whom they feel safe. We can be safe and tough at the same time.

Life Principle—Who Is My Safe Place?

We all need someone we can go to who is a safe place, someone whom we can trust. Someone who is kind. We all need someone who speaks wisdom and truth into our lives. Someone wiser. Someone who can listen and be a mentor.

I am a parent and a husband and a boss. I need to be a safe place for my kids and for my wife. I need to be a safe place for my employees at work. This means that I care for them, that I don't lash out in anger or take out my disappointments on them, that I don't try to even scores or condemn them, or give up on them. It means that I think about what is best for them. Sometimes that may be tough love and sometimes it may be unexplainable amazing grace. I need to apologize when I cross the line.

In order to be a safe place, I need a safe place. I am fortunate to have a kind wife who is safe. My parents are safe. My best friends are safe. Just ask yourself: When I need a safe place, to whom do I go?

Folks who don't have a "safe place someone" tend to hide or escape. Some escape to anger and violence, some escape to a bottle, some escape to the mall, some escape to chocolate, some escape to work, to sex, or to the local pool hall.

It is worth the effort to find someone who is a safe place.

Jesus Principle—Jesus Is the Safest Place

Of all my safe places, I have found that Jesus is my safest place. The Jesus I read about in scripture loved me enough to die in order to pay the penalty I should have paid. He opened the door to His Father so I could approach God Himself like a little child. Jesus is a friend who sticks closer than a brother: He keeps me from condemnation, He gives me the faith to believe in Him, He shares His inheritance with me, He knows me through and through, and He accepts me and wants the best for me.

When I am in difficult times, I know I can go to Him and spill my heart, ask for advice, ask for divine intervention, and give Him my cares. I know that while He may challenge me and stretch me and lead me in and through difficult waters, He will never do anything to hurt me, tear me down permanently, or condemn me or judge me. There is no safe place like Him.

THIRTY-FIVE

CHAMPION

Football Principle—To Be a Champion On and Off the Field

Some things just don't go together. I love both peanut butter and sausage pizza, but I have never been tempted to put the two together. I dated a few girls for way too long even after I knew we didn't really go together. Nothing against them, but the dating relationship should have scaled back to a friendship sooner when it was clear we weren't going to spend a lifetime together.

Similarly, just as not all things go together, not all things naturally follow. Ed "Too Tall" Jones was an amazing football player for the Dallas Cowboys, but that did not make him an amazing boxer. Michael Jordan, one of the greatest basketball players of all time, tried his hand at professional baseball and fell far short of his accolades on the basketball court. Just because someone is very good and perhaps the best at one thing, doesn't mean that they will be any good at another thing.

There are plenty of great athletes who get into trouble in their personal lives because it doesn't naturally follow that a great player is a great life-doer. The problem is that bad performance off the field often catches up with us on the field. The distractions caused by travails off the field cause the athlete and his team to suffer. We have had to suspend some of our best players for bad grades. It starts early in life and bad habits are difficult to replace.

Because of previous experiences with bad performers off the field, many teams now focus on good integrity when they draft, recruit, and pick starting players. Integrity means you are consistent in all areas of your life, whether or not there is a big crowd in the stands. The bottom line is that a coach would much rather have an athlete who is consistently good off the field—one who knows how to get along with people, has self-control, respects the person and property of others, feels some responsibility to his fellow man, and loves good works. This person makes a better teammate and challenges others to be better teammates, husbands, fathers, children, supervisors, and so forth.

In the long term, I believe those who are champions off the field make more of a lasting difference in this world than those who are merely champions on the field. When I refer to champions on the field, I mean those who play consistently at high levels, make a positive difference in the game for their team, and have won at a high level. You don't have to be famous to be a champion.

The advantage that these on-the-field champions have is that they know what it takes to be a champion—hard work, sacrifice, determination, dedication, commitment, and guidance. Becoming a champion off the field requires the same thing. Being a champion off the field must be a priority in our lives if we are to win in life by leaving a trail of good works and positive influence behind us.

Life Principle— Use Your Champion Life Abilities in the Areas That Really Matter

Not all of us have the skill sets or abilities to know what it feels like to be a champion on the football field, but all of us are good at something. There is something that each of us can say, "This is my best skill...." It may be work, investing, creating, building, selling, promoting, managing, or any number of other skills. We know that our best skill didn't just happen overnight. It took time, focus, sacrifice, interest, learning, emotions, energy, and resources.

It would be great if our best skill lined up well with the things in life that are most important. Besides throwing a football, one of my best skills seems to be the ability to work really hard. That skill did not come naturally for me. (Naturally, sometimes I think I would rather sit on the couch and eat chips.) It took time, perseverance, focus, and drive. It required patience and diligent effort and a belief that I could do better. I learned most of this in the context of my vocation. However, over the years, I have realized that being successful in my vocation doesn't necessarily mean that I am a good husband, father, friend, or leader.

Being a good husband, father, friend, and leader is important to me because the internal reward is greater, the effect is longer lasting (generations), and frankly, the challenge is greater. I might erroneously think that I could pay my wife to stay with me, but I certainly can't pay her to admire and respect me and be on the same page with me. The same is true for my kids and friends and those I lead.

If I were really smart, I would take what I know is required to be a hard worker (time, energy, patience, diligence) and apply those to being a better husband, father, friend, and leader.

Jesus Principle—Jesus Is Our Champion

Just as those who are champions on the field have an advantage, so do those who have Jesus in their heart, who have received Him, who believe that He is the Son of God and died and rose again. Jesus is our champion. He championed over sin and death on the cross and gave His life in love to us. Each day we can faithfully surrender ourselves to Him to become His conduit, an instrument in His hands, and leave a trail of good works. In doing so, we are a champion on the field of life.

Amen.

THIRTY-SIX
CELEBRATE

Football Principle—Is Celebration Part of Your Game? Do You Have a Good Touchdown Dance?

Is it fair to say most guys don't like to dance? It can feel awkward to wiggle your body in different directions in front of people. This feeling is especially true if your wife pulls you out to be the first one on the dance floor at weddings and at your high school reunion. Do I sound like I have been embarrassed before?

After a touchdown, it almost doesn't matter how crazy you look. Your team and your fans are so excited, you can almost do no wrong. So, you might as well be free and let it go. Be creative, enthusiastic, and awesome. We have seen some really cool and "interesting" touchdown (TD) dances over the years. Deion Sanders' touchdown dance sticks out in my mind. The touchdown dance is just a fun way to celebrate after a score.

I am thankful we were given the capability to celebrate good things. It is a natural response to something really awesome. It completes the awesomeness. Can you imagine what it would be like if you won a Super Bowl but couldn't celebrate? It is hard to imagine walking off the field with no emotion, no hugs, no confetti, no music, no crazy fans, no circling the field ... none of that. What would the postgame interviews be like? All that bottled-up joy and nothing to do with it. That doesn't seem right. It would be similar to how an animal behaves when it wins a competition. The losers and winners at the dog show don't behave much differently. We are definitely made differently than animals. Again, I am thankful for that.

A coach wants his players to celebrate a great play to complete the joy of the moment, but of course not in a way that loses sight of the task at hand. The celebration should be awesome and be a contributor to the momentum of the game.

Life Principle—Learn to Celebrate ... Together

A great friend of mine runs a ministry called All Pro Dad. Their vision is to help family members love each other well. One of the things they do to accomplish that vision is to put on events at NFL and college stadiums for dads and their sons to attend. Fathers and sons rotate through different stations where they learn a little football and a little about life in a fun way. One of my favorite stations is the touchdown dance. Each dad starts at the 5-yard line, takes a handoff, runs into the end zone with the ball, and then does his craziest TD dance. Then the kids do it. It is crazy fun. And what happens in a real game after the dance? Players hug and chest bump. At the All Pro Dad day, the dad and son are encouraged to hug. Some of these dads have never hugged their son. Some cry. Some don't want to let go. Celebration can be healing.

Jesus Principle—Jesus Celebrates Us. Do We Celebrate Him?

Scripture says that when someone comes to Christ, the angels and the heavens celebrate (Luke 15:10). What a scene that must be.

The other day a friend of mine told me that maybe Jesus is coming back soon. I asked my family, "What would you do if you knew He was coming back sometime in the next few months?" My answer was that I wanted to be prepared to praise Him as He deserves to be praised. I wanted to be able to celebrate Him in the most full way with all of my being. I want my soul to be able to sing and dance to celebrate the one who is most special to me. I started thinking—I don't want any of this celebration to be fake. I want it to be a continuation of what is already happening in my heart on a daily basis. I want to allow Jesus to work in me to create a fullness. I want to appreciate His gifts to me—His mercy, His salvation, His friendship, His brotherhood—and let my cup run over. I want to experience daily what I believe the songwriters experienced as they expressed their celebration when they wrote "Amazing Grace" and "How Great Thou Art." When I see Him, I want to continue the celebration and I want to look forward to that day when I can praise Him with my full heart without being held back by my humanity.

Take a look at JointheApplause.com.

THIRTY-SEVEN
ANTICIPATION

Football Principle—Preparation Leads to Anticipation

The "Pick Six" is one of the coolest plays in football. It is one of the few plays that has its own expression—Pick Six. What a thrill it must be for the defense and especially the player who is in the right place at the right time to intercept a pass and "take it to the house" for six points.

Sometimes the opportunity to make a Pick Six is a gift that requires no anticipation by the defender, but most of the time, this great play is a result of great anticipation. It is impossible to anticipate well without a strong knowledge and understanding of the game, the situation, and the opponent. The best defenders know their opponents sometimes better than they know themselves. These defenders understand the keys and tendencies and unique movements of their opponents. This understanding comes from hours in the film room, the development of a plan of defense, and practicing the execution of that plan.

We have all experienced this in some form or fashion. It is always easier to anticipate my opponent the more I play against that person or team.

I have a friend who works for a worldwide accounting firm. He has the dream job of studying game film and breaking it down for NFL teams. His report helps his client's coaches and players know their opponents better. His scouting report details tendencies, weaknesses, and strengths, all for the purpose of developing and executing a game plan, in large part based on the anticipation of what the other team will do.

The team that prepares well enough to anticipate puts itself in the best position to win.

Life Principle—Overcome Adversity by Anticipating

I am not a litigator, but I do negotiate business contracts. To negotiate well on my client's behalf, it is important for me to be able to anticipate how the opposing attorney might object to my requests to make changes in the contract that might help my client and be adverse to his client. My ability to anticipate is directly related to how well I understand the contract and the nuances of the business interest being represented by opposing counsel. It is hard work and takes a lot of time to understand my opponent's business, but it pays off for my client when I anticipate the objections and prepare in advance to overcome those objections.

It is no different than what salespeople do. They prepare well to understand their customers. They use this understanding to anticipate objections and then prepare to overcome them and make the sale.

The same thing is true when we are following our dreams or reaching toward a goal. We will encounter adversity. We must anticipate this adversity and be prepared to respond. One way of doing this is to ask ourselves and others all the "what-ifs." The "what-ifs" lead to understanding and greater anticipation and better responses to adversity, and ultimately a more efficient path to our goals.

Jesus Principle—Jesus Anticipates the Day He Comes for His Bride

It is written in Scripture that no one knows the day of Jesus' second coming, but that it is good to assume it is near and to anticipate His coming (Matt. 24:36, 42–44).

Let's look at this from Jesus' angle, though. Can you imagine how much anticipation Jesus has to come back and meet us, His bride, and take us home and fully glorify us and live with us forever?

He said that He went to heaven to prepare a place for us. He has done and continues to do so much to prepare for that day. He lived a human life so that He could empathize with us. He died to forgive sin and reconcile us to His Father. He defeated death and rose to life again. He sent His Spirit to live in us, to guide us into truth, and to bring us closer to Him.

He knows us through and through. He continues His work for us and in us in anticipation of that day. It seems well worth it to Him. He wants to be able to present us unblemished, and He will. What a glorious day that will be!

THIRTY-EIGHT
BATTLE

Football Principle—Are We Executing the Battle Plan?

Years ago I attended a Dallas Cowboys game. It was my first pro game where I had seats close enough to smell the sweat and hear the hits. I was amazed at how fast the game was and how intense the contact was. It was war out there. Every play was a battle. The time between the whistles was time to prepare for the next battle. Time-outs were called to give a little extra time to prepare for the next series of battles or to care for the injured.

In football, each battle lasts approximately six seconds. During that six seconds, the outcome of the war can be determined. Each battle has a battle plan for the players to carry out. Different plans are used for different situations. Some plans are conservative, and others are risky. All battle plans are designed to establish dominance, to keep the other side off balance, to take them out of their overall battle plan, and to ultimately win the game. Often the plan makes the difference, but no plan can make the difference without the players executing the plan.

Some may think each battle goes to the stronger, bigger, and faster team. That might be the safer bet, but the difference in a game is often the result of who wins the battle between the ears and in the heart.

Focus, understanding, determination, and willpower often dominate the battle and win the war. You can't actually see focus, understanding, determination, and willpower like you can see strength and speed, but you can see their results. Likewise, you can't see fear, impatience, or lack of trust, but you can see the results of those character flaws.

For example, we have all seen countless plays where a player doesn't do his job because he doesn't trust another player. I see defensive players leaving their gaps to cover another one. I see offensive linemen moving out of position. I see receivers breaking off routes and running backs not trusting the hole will be there. I see QBs not believing the receiver will make the right cut on time. These battles involving the heart are the tougher ones to fight. They are certainly more difficult to diagnose and to cure. These diseases of heart character spread and must be diagnosed and taken care of before they become an epidemic. Sometimes the medicine will be uncomfortable, but it must be administered for any player and any team to excel.

Life Principle—Pick Your Battles and Not Every One at That

The character traits revealed in football also play out in how we live our lives. We are all a mixture of good and bad character traits. Whether good or bad, they need to be identified and managed. We all have different backgrounds, too. I am not sure which shapes which— the character traits or the life experiences—or maybe there is some combination of both. In any event, the mixture of the two results in opinions, values, beliefs, perceptions, attitudes, behavior, and the like. Since my mixture is different from the mixture of others, then my opinions, values, and such are different from everyone else, some more than others. When you mix all of mankind on one globe, guess what comes next—potential disputes, judgments, offensive and defensive actions, battles, and even wars. Needless to say, we could spend all day fighting if we wanted to. Some appear to want to. As for me, as much as possible, I like to live at peace with all men and women. So, if you are anything like me, we have to learn to pick our battles.

How do I pick my battles? Clearly, I am, as a husband and a father, the shield for my wife and my children. I am the one there to protect them emotionally, physically, intellectually, and spiritually. I am, as an employer, a protector of my employees and as a friend, a protector of my friends. I also feel called to battle for those in need and to help folks, who want to, battle against harmful thinking.

The irony is that those I am around the most and to whom I have a greater duty of protection—family and friends—are the very ones I am tempted to battle with more than others. Also, every now and then, I am tempted to pick out a group of folks to dislike or even despise, but, given my long list of imperfections, I don't think that I have any right to do so.

The biggest mistake I can make is to believe my battle is against a person, whether it be my wife, my kids, my friends, my employees, or just simple acquaintances. My real battle is not against the child who defies doing homework, a family member who can't admit they are wrong or say they are sorry, a business partner who takes liberties with joint property, a child who lies, or a family member who embarrasses the family. Rather, my real battle is against the heart and mind behind the bad behavior.

With this in mind and for the good of all involved, I must pick battles where I believe the other person, or perhaps our relationship, is headed down the wrong path. These are battles where the end result is not forever condemnation or punishment, but rather a course correction, rescue, redemption, and restoration. I must fight the battle that results in the best interests of all those involved. With this focus, the battle plan is different than one that wants to establish dominance or invoke punishment. This battle plan is one that is best for all.

Jesus Principle—Our Battle Is Not against Flesh and Blood

When I pick a battle, I need to remind myself of Ephesians 6:12, which says that my battle is not against flesh and blood but against spirits and powers of darkness. I must battle not against a person but against the spirits of laziness, apathy, disrespect, defiance, pride, selfishness, emptiness, loneliness, and anger. I must separate the person from the sin. I must battle while loving the person and hating the sin. Loving the person but battling against the sin is kind of like fighting to get the item you despise taken off the menu at your favorite restaurant. You love the restaurant but there is something on the menu that needs to be rethought and replaced.

God does the same with us. He loved us while we were His enemies and offered to us His life as a replacement for ours, and with that a new way of thinking. He won the battle against sin and death and offers us new thoughts and new character traits to replace those that are harmful to us and to others. We use weapons of His truth to fight the battles against the unseen spirits of destruction.

This battle plan is already laid out in scripture, and its main weapon is love. We merely need to believe and execute.

THIRTY-NINE
SHAKE IT OFF

Football Principle—Shake It Off

Sometimes as fans, we are angry when a player doesn't immediately show remorse or regret for the horrible mistake he just made. We want the guy to suffer because he made us suffer. We want him to account for his mistake. I have seen fans yell obscenities at players who seemed oblivious to the onslaught and who seemed to care little about the mistake they just made.

As a coach, I want my athlete at his best every play. I know we will deal with mistakes later in practice and in the film room in order to learn, but during the game I want my player fully engaged in the next play. We can't be fully engaged in the next play if we are beating ourselves up for the mistake we just made on the previous play. As coaches, we say things like: "Forget about it," "Shake it off," or "The team needs you at one hundred percent."

Being able to shake it off is a learned skill. If we can't learn that skill, we will never reach our potential. We will make mistakes—no ifs, ands, or buts. We can't climb the mountain nearly as high if we are carrying a bag full of regret and condemnation for ourselves. That stuff gets really heavy. We can't play the game if we are in the penalty box.

Life Principle—Learn and Move On

If someone comes to you for advice and says, "My life is a wreck. I have made so many horrible mistakes and I feel so burdened that I am not sure I will ever make it," what would you say? Would you say, "Tell me about all your mistakes," and afterward say, "Wow, you are right, those mistakes are too much to overcome"? More likely you would say something like, "I am happy to hear all that you have done wrong and all that is weighing you down, but when you are finished, I am going to say, 'We can't redo the past, but we can learn from it, change the way we think about it, and focus on the present and the future. And I can help you with that, because I have had to do it myself.'" We have "responsibility"—the ability to respond in different ways. We can choose to bury ourselves deeper or learn and move on thankful for another day.

Jesus Principle—Staying Out of the Penalty Box Is an Act of Faith That Pleases God

God says He forgets our sins, because of the wonderful work of Jesus on the cross. Not just forgiven, but also forgotten. What good does it do for God to remember sin that He has promised not to condemn us for? If God does not remember or condemn us for our sin, then what right do we have to remember and condemn ourselves? Are we higher than God?

Of course, it is difficult to actually forget our big mistakes, but we can learn to place the condemnation for the mistake on Jesus (just as God did) and then be thankful for that provision from God. Having gratitude for not being condemned leads us away from sin. The world does not stop the consequences that flow from our mistakes, but God has provided a way to be right with Him regardless of our mistakes and to feel His forgiveness so that we can stay in the game He has given us to play.

My wife and I led a small group for a while. There was a couple in the small group who spoke up one night to say that because of something that had happened in the past, they felt unworthy to take communion or otherwise get involved in the church. My response was, "Can you name a sin that Christ did not die for? If He does not condemn you, then why should you condemn yourselves?" The light came on for them that night and it was a blessing to me. The Lord has given me other opportunities to ask that question and it always thrills my soul to share the good news that no matter what has happened we can still be engaged in all God has for us without condemnation or fear of retribution from our loving Father. Wow!!!

FORTY
TOGETHER

Football Principle—There Is Something about a Really Good Huddle

A huddle is a place where the team comes together before a play to make sure everyone knows the plan of attack for the next play. I like a really good huddle. It bothers me when I see a team with a disjointed, disorganized huddle, with players barely leaning in and some not even looking at the quarterback. The body language of a disjointed huddle says to me, "I don't care about my teammates, we aren't really a team, and what we are doing right now is not important."

Forming a huddle can be a great teaching tool for the fundamentals of unity and togetherness and being a true team. Whose voice do we listen to? How do we show that we are a team and not just a crowd on a street corner? How do we show consideration and respect for our teammates? How do we show that we are truly in this together? How do we break the huddle with the force of one? How do we show we know what we are doing? How do we show we care about the little things that can make us great? How do we show that we are disciplined? I am told Bear Bryant practiced making a huddle for two full days at the beginning of every season.

It can seem a little silly sometimes when you see mature, three-hundred-pound men holding hands in a huddle, but I can guarantee you it puts the other team on their heels before the ball is ever snapped. The discipline and joy of unity convey power and might.

As a coach and a teammate, we need to do things that create community and togetherness in our teams—things that convey discipline and unity.

And when we say, "Let's do this!" we need to find ways to emphasize the "*Let's*" part. The huddle is a great place to start.

Life Principle—True Success Can't Be Defined without Meaningful Relationships

We generally think of isolation as a penalty for bad performance. Kids are put in time-out, hockey players go to the penalty box, football players get benched, and employees are fired.

Isolation can also result from life circumstances and intentional decisions. Kids and spouses are abandoned, kids are pinpointed and bullied into a dark place, and we sometimes bully ourselves by playing the comparison game or with haunting regrets, or we simply give up on ourselves and others.

Isolation can also result from what some might call success. There is a form of isolation of the soul that results from climbing the ladder and leaving others behind, thinking that if we can get to the top of the ladder or near it, then our soul will be satisfied. It has been documented over and over the number of millionaires and billionaires who seem to have it all on the outside, but who feel trapped, imprisoned, isolated, and empty on the inside. There is nothing wrong with climbing a ladder, unless it is done at the expense of meaningful relationships with others.

The problem is that our soul was made in such a way that it can't be satisfied by things or accomplishments. Sure, there is a temporary fulfillment when we get to the top of the ladder, but we soon find out it doesn't last.

Our soul was made for community, to love and care for, and to be loved and cared for. These are the things that are eternal and can be attained without climbing a ladder. These are the things that fight isolation and bring meaning and satisfaction to our souls.

As a lawyer, my greatest satisfaction has come from helping others and caring for others personally, and allowing others to help me and care for me. I will never forget what my law firm did for me early on when my family was in a tough spot. At the direction of the chairman, my firm went well beyond what I was worth to the firm (as a young associate) to help rescue my dad.

A soul that is isolated from giving love and care to others is not rescued by more money in the bank. A soul that does life in a meaningful way with others is healthy and powerful to bring love and care to others and to receive love, to be satisfied, and to make an eternal difference in the world.

What would our lives look like if we focused more on meaningful relationships? Can you name one or two relationships in your life that don't depend on or contribute to making money?

Jesus Principle—Jesus Is the Way to the Most Meaningful Relationship of All

If you had to rank your relationship with God, your relationship with others, and your relationship with yourself, which one would you say is the easiest? Which one is the hardest?

Until I was twenty-six, I would have said that the easiest relationship was with others and by far the hardest would be my relationship with God. You see, I viewed God as someone who looked down on me when I didn't measure up to His standards. The problem was, despite trying so hard, I really never felt as though I measured up. I felt that I had to earn His approval and bargain for forgiveness and favor. These are not good things to feel in a relationship, especially one you want to be meaningful.

Thankfully, God rescued me and taught me through the book of Romans that all the approval, measuring up, and forgiveness I had been trying to earn had already been earned for me by the work of Jesus. When I finally received that truth by faith, I decided to let God love me and care for me. I began to feel accepted and loved by God, and it paved the way for a meaningful, thankful relationship with Him —the most important relationship in my life.

Is anything standing in your way, keeping you from having a meaningful relationship with God? If so, can you describe it? Can you research the Scriptures to see if what you are believing is true?

FINAL NOTE FROM COACH RANDY

I hope you have been able to connect some of the truths I have shared with your journey. And, I hope you will help others understand and connect with these truths.

May God's goodness and mercy follow you all the days of your life.

And a huge thank you to my wife, Jennifer, and my kids, Ellie (and her husband Michael), JR (and his wife Morgan), Julia, Katya and Alec, and so many friends who encouraged me to the task to get this done. Also a huge thanks to my players who care so much. I am forever grateful.

Love, Randy